Reading & Writing
Taj Mahal

NATIONAL GEOGRAPHIC
L E A R N I N G

Australia • Brazil • Mexico • Singapore • United Kingdom • United States

National Geographic Learning,
a Cengage Company

Reading & Writing, Taj Mahal

**Lauri Blass, Mari Vargo, Keith S. Folse,
April Muchmore-Vokoun, Elena Vestri**

Publisher: Sherrise Roehr

Executive Editor: Laura LeDréan

Managing Editor: Jennifer Monaghan

Digital Implementation Manager,
Irene Boixareu

Senior Media Researcher: Leila Hishmeh

Director of Global Marketing: Ian Martin

Regional Sales and National Account
Manager: Andrew O'Shea

Content Project Manager: Ruth Moore

Senior Designer: Lisa Trager

Manufacturing Planner: Mary Beth
Hennebury

Composition: Lumina Datamatics

For permission to use material from this text or product,
submit all requests online at **cengage.com/permissions**
Further permissions questions can be emailed to
permissionrequest@cengage.com

Student Edition: Reading & Writing, Taj Mahal
ISBN-13: 978-0-357-13832-8

National Geographic Learning
20 Channel Center Street
Boston, MA 02210
USA

Locate your local office at **international.cengage.com/region**

Visit National Geographic Learning online at **ELTNGL.com**
Visit our corporate website at **www.cengage.com**

Printed in the United States of America
Print Number: 03   Print Year: 2022

PHOTO CREDITS

Scope and Sequence

MEMORY AND LEARNING

Artist Stephen Wiltshire
sketches the New York City
skyline from memory.

THINK AND DISCUSS

1   What is your earliest memory?
2   Why do you think some people have better
    memories than others?

EXPLORE THE THEME

A **Look at the photo for 30 seconds and answer the questions.**

1. How many items can you remember? Close your book and make a list.

2. Compare lists with a partner. Who remembered more items correctly? Were some items easier to remember than others?

B **What does the graph on the next page show about how memory changes with age?**

C **Match the correct form of the words in blue to their definitions.**

_____ (n) a special way of doing something

_____ (adv) slowly and in small stages or amounts

_____ (adj) having parts that connect or go together in complicated ways

HOW WE REMEMBER

The brain is the most **complex** organ in the human body. It has about 100 billion nerve cells, or neurons. We make memories when connections are made between the brain's neurons. The more connections there are, the easier it is to recall information.

Memories about childhood and things that happened long ago are called long-term memories. Telephone numbers and the names of people we just met are stored in our brains as short-term memories.

There are certain **techniques** we can use to improve memory. However, as the graph shows, our ability to remember—or recall—things **gradually** worsens over time. This is because, as we age, connections between neurons weaken or are lost.

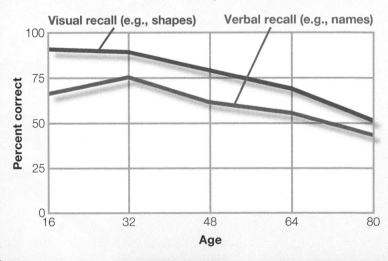

Adult Ability to Recall

Visual recall (e.g., shapes)   Verbal recall (e.g., names)

Percent correct

100
75
50
25
0

16   32   48   64   80

Age

Reading 1

PREPARING TO READ

BUILDING
VOCABULARY

A The words in blue below are used in the reading passage on pages 5–6. Complete each sentence with the correct word. Use a dictionary to help you.

> familiar   visualize   memorize   external   text   achievement   internal

1. If something looks _____ to you, you recognize it or know it well.

2. A(n) _____ is a book or other written or printed work.

3. Things that exist inside a particular person, object, or place are _____.

4. Things that exist outside a particular person, object, or place are _____.

5. When you _____ something, you form a picture of it in your mind.

6. To _____ means to learn something so that you will remember it exactly.

7. A(n) _____ is something that is done successfully, especially after a lot of effort.

USING
VOCABULARY

B Discuss these questions with a partner.
1. What places are you **familiar** with? Describe a place that you know well.
2. What **external** conditions make it difficult for you to study?

CLASSIFYING

C Do you ever make lists to remember things? Do you ever try to memorize things? Complete the chart below. Then compare your answers with a partner.

Things I make lists for	Things I try to memorize

PREDICTING

D Scan the reading passage on pages 5–6 quickly. List two other nouns or verbs that appear two or more times.

_____*memory*_____   _____   _____

Now look at the words you wrote. What do you think the reading passage is about? Share your ideas with a partner. Then check your ideas as you read the passage.

In the BBC series *Sherlock*, detective Sherlock Holmes—played by Benedict Cumberbatch—uses the loci method to recall information.

THE ART OF MEMORY

🎧 Track 1

A   We all try to remember certain things in our daily lives: telephone numbers, email addresses, facts that we learn in class, and important tasks. We use memory techniques like repetition—the idea that the more we repeat a piece of information, the better we can recall it. But did you know that memory training goes all the way back to the days of ancient Greece?

B   People began to value memory as a skill about 2,500 years ago. That's when the Greek poet Simonides of Ceos came up with a powerful technique known as the loci[1] method. Simonides realized that it's easier to remember places and locations than it is to remember lists of names. According to the loci method, if you think of a very familiar place and visualize certain things in that place, then you can keep those things in your memory for a long time.

C   Simonides called this imagined place a "memory palace." Your memory palace can be any place that you know well, such as your home or your school. Here's how to use the loci method to remember a list of tasks: Let's say your memory palace is based on your house. Visualize yourself walking through it. Imagine yourself doing each task in a different room. Later, when you want to recall your list of tasks, visualize yourself walking through your house again. You will remember your list of tasks as you see yourself doing each one.

[1] Loci is the plural form of the Latin noun *locus*, meaning "place."

In the 15th century, an Italian man named Peter of Ravenna used the loci method to **memorize** books and poems. He memorized religious **texts**, 200 speeches, all of the laws of that time, and 1,000 poems. By using the loci method, he was able to "read" books stored in his memory palaces. "When I [travel] I can truly say I carry everything I own with me," he wrote.

When Simonides and Peter of Ravenna were alive, most people did not have books or pens to write notes with. They had to remember what they learned. In her book titled *The Book of Memory*, Mary Carruthers writes about these memory techniques of the past. She explains that ancient people considered memory to be a great virtue.[2] A person with a good memory was special because they could help preserve the society's cultural heritage.[3]

After Simonides developed the loci method, other people continued to study the art of memory. Memorization gained a **complex** set of rules and instructions. Students of memory learned what to remember and techniques for how to remember it. In fact, memory training is still an important activity in many parts of the world today. In some cultures, memorizing religious texts is considered a great **achievement**. Other cultures value people who can tell myths and folktales from the past, as there is often no written record of these things.

Over the past millennium,[4] though, many things have changed. We've **gradually** replaced our **internal** memory with **external** memory. We've invented devices so we don't have to store information in our brains. We now have photographs to record our experiences, calendars to keep track of our schedules, and the Internet and computers to store our ideas. As a result, we've gone from remembering many things to remembering very little. Nowadays, when we want to know something, we just look it up. But how does this affect us and our society? Did we lose an important skill?

[2] A **virtue** is a very good personal quality.
[3] **Heritage** is something that is handed down from the past (e.g., a society's traditions, achievements, and beliefs).
[4] A **millennium** is a period of one thousand years.

▼ Competitors memorize names and faces at the World Memory Championships, London.

UNDERSTANDING THE READING

A Choose the best alternative title for the reading passage.

UNDERSTANDING
THE MAIN IDEA

    a. Modern Memory Techniques
    b. Memorization Throughout History
    c. Internal and External Memory

B Answer the questions below using information from the reading passage.

UNDERSTANDING
DETAILS

    1. What is the loci method? Explain it in your own words.

    _____

    2. What benefit did the loci method have for Peter of Ravenna?

    _____

    3. According to Mary Carruthers, why was memory so important in the past?

    _____

    4. What is one example of the important role of memory in certain cultures today?

    _____

C Read the list of memory techniques and devices below. If the item relates to internal memory, circle **I**. If it relates to external memory, circle **E**.

CLASSIFYING

1. repetition	I	E
2. books	I	E
3. photographs	I	E
4. loci method	I	E
5. tablet computers	I	E

> **CRITICAL THINKING** **Applying information**, such as a method or procedure, can help you internalize it more easily. For example, using the loci method yourself will help you understand the concept and remember how it works.

D Imagine you have these problems. How might you solve them by using the loci method? Share your ideas with a partner.

CRITICAL THINKING:
APPLYING A METHOD

    1. You are learning a foreign language. You are having trouble remembering new words.
    2. You are taking a history class. It's hard for you to remember when important events happened and the names of the people involved.

E The author writes:

CRITICAL THINKING:
REFLECTING

We've gradually replaced our internal memory with external memory. … We've gone from remembering many things to remembering very little.

Do you think we have lost an important skill? Why or why not? Discuss with a partner and give examples from your own lives.

MEMORY AND LEARNING 7

DEVELOPING READING SKILLS

READING SKILL   Identifying Cause and Effect

A **cause** is something that makes another event happen. The resulting event is the **effect**. Recognizing causes and effects can help you better understand a reading passage. Look at the sentence below. Does the underlined portion show a cause or an effect?

> *If you think of a very familiar place and visualize certain things in that place, then you can keep those things in your memory for a long time.*

The underlined portion shows the effect. Visualizing things within a familiar place is the cause. Keeping memories for a long time is the effect.

You can sometimes identify cause-and-effect relationships by finding certain connecting or signal words. These include *because, so, if … then, therefore, as a result,* and *by* verb + *-ing.*

> *We don't have to remember phone numbers now **because** we can store them in our cell phones.*

> *I enter my email password three times a day, **so** I remember it easily.*

IDENTIFYING CAUSE
AND EFFECT

A Read the information about memorization techniques. How many cause-effect relationships can you find? Circle the causes and underline their effects.

Techniques for remembering things like lists, numbers, and facts are called mnemonic devices. People often use mnemonics—like poems or pictures—because it's easier to remember rhymes or images than plain facts and lists.

Acronyms are one type of mnemonic. For example, it may be hard to remember the colors of the rainbow in the order that they appear. Someone therefore made an acronym for this: ROY G BIV. The letters in the acronym are the first letters in the names for the colors: red, orange, yellow, green, blue, indigo, and violet. The name Roy G. Biv is meaningless, but it's short, so it's easier to remember than the list.

English spelling rules can also be difficult to learn, so some students use rhymes to help them remember the rules. By learning "*i* before *e* except after *c* (where you hear *ee*)," students of English can remember the spelling of words like *niece* and *receipt*.

IDENTIFYING CAUSE
AND EFFECT

B Look back at the reading passage on pages 5–6. Circle three causes and underline their effects.

Video

HOUSE OF CARDS

▲ **Nelson Dellis is a four-time USA Memory Champion.**

BEFORE VIEWING

A Read the information about the USA Memory Championship. Then answer the questions.

LEARNING ABOUT THE TOPIC

The USA Memory Championship is an annual competition in which participants compete in memorization tasks. In one event, participants have to memorize the order of a shuffled[1] deck of cards. First, they are given five minutes to memorize the order of the cards. Then they are given five minutes to arrange a second deck of cards in the same order. The participant who recalls all the cards correctly in the shortest time period wins.

[1]If a deck of cards is **shuffled**, the cards are mixed up in a random order.

1. What do you think the record time for the card event is? Note your answer. Then check the answer on the bottom of page 20. Does this surprise you?

   _____

2. How might a person use the loci method to memorize the order of a deck of cards?

   _____

B The words and phrases in **bold** below are used in the video. Match each word or phrase to its definition.

VOCABULARY IN CONTEXT

> People often **code** information by using mnemonic devices, like poems or pictures.
>
> Information is easier to recall if it has an **associated** rhyme or image.
>
> Most people have a **mental map** of their home or neighborhood.

1. _____ (n) a picture in a person's mind of an area

2. _____ (adj) connected with something else

3. _____ (v) to give a name, number, or symbol to something

WHILE VIEWING

UNDERSTANDING MAIN IDEAS

A ▶ Watch the video. How does Nelson Dellis memorize the cards? Order the steps (a–e). Two sentences are extra.

Step 1: _____ Step 2: _____ Step 3: _____

a. He groups three cards at a time to create brief stories.
b. He connects each card to someone familiar, with an associated action and object.
c. He groups the whole deck of cards into four piles.
d. He counts the number of cards in each pile.
e. He places the images around a familiar mental map in his mind.

UNDERSTANDING DETAILS

B ▶ Watch the video again. Complete the labels in Dellis's memory palace below. Then draw a line connecting each label (2–4) to the correct image. See the example provided.

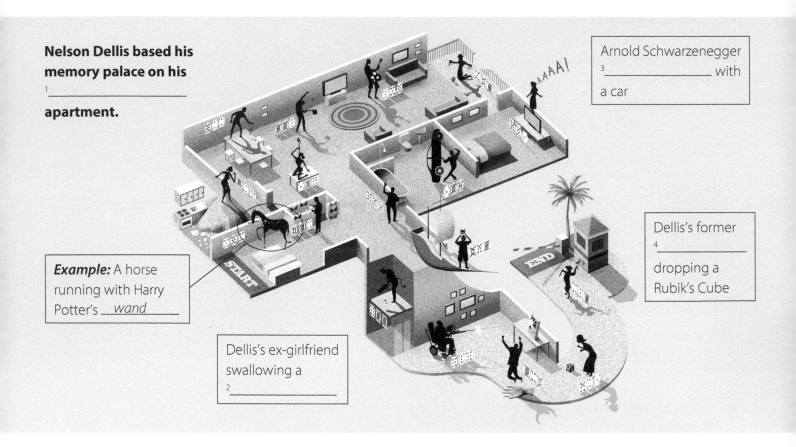

Nelson Dellis based his memory palace on his
1 _____
apartment.

Arnold Schwarzenegger
3 _____ with a car

Example: A horse running with Harry Potter's ___*wand*___

Dellis's former
4 _____
dropping a Rubik's Cube

Dellis's ex-girlfriend swallowing a
2 _____

AFTER VIEWING

REACTING TO THE VIDEO

A Many images in Dellis's memory palace are very strange or unusual. Why do you think this is? Discuss with a partner.

CRITICAL THINKING: APPLYING A METHOD

B Imagine you are at a party and you have to memorize the names of 20 people. What method or system would you use? Share your ideas with a partner.

Reading 2

PREPARING TO READ

A The words in blue below are used in the reading passage on pages 12–13. Read their definitions and then complete each sentence with the correct form of the word.

BUILDING VOCABULARY

> A **mental** activity uses and exercises the mind.
>
> A **physical** activity uses and exercises the body.
>
> If you have **proof**, you have evidence that shows something is true.
>
> A **route** is a way or path taken to get from one place to another.
>
> A **drug** is a chemical intended to affect the structure or function of the body.
>
> If you are experiencing **stress**, you are worried about problems in your life.
>
> To **transfer** something means to move it from one place to another.
>
> A person's **state** refers to the condition they are in at a certain time.

1. Scientists can give a rat a _____ to make it go to sleep or stay awake.

2. Doing a _____ activity such as a crossword puzzle can improve memory.

3. Because of a recent study, we now have _____ that sleep is important for memory.

4. A person in a _____ of confusion isn't sure what is happening.

5. If a student is under too much _____, they may perform badly.

6. Research shows that regular _____ activity—such as cycling or dancing—has significant benefits for memory.

7. Storing phone numbers in cell phones is an example of _____ information from internal to external memory.

8. People with a good sense of direction are good at remembering _____.

B Discuss these questions with a partner.

USING VOCABULARY

1. What kinds of **physical** activities do you enjoy doing? Why?
2. Which **routes** do you find easy to remember? Which routes are harder to memorize? Why do you think this is?

C Underline the key words in the title and the subheads of the reading passage on pages 12–13. Use the underlined words to help you complete the sentence below. Then check your answer as you read the passage.

PREDICTING

I think the reading passage is about _____

_____

SLEEP AND MEMORY

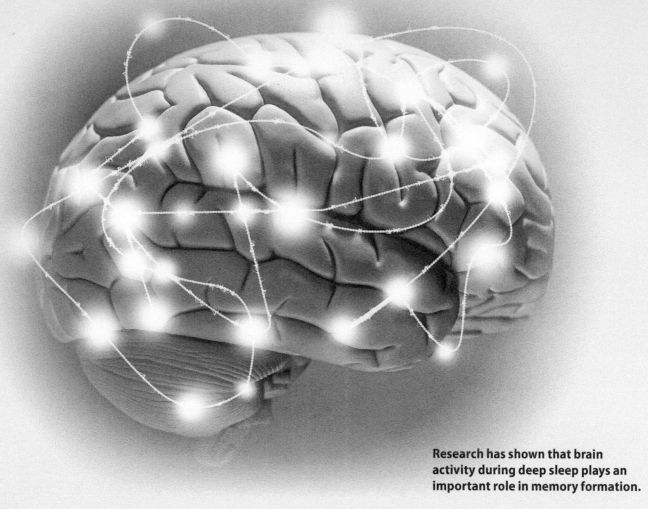

Research has shown that brain activity during deep sleep plays an important role in memory formation.

Track 2

A Many people think that sleep must be important for memory, but until recently there was little proof. Scientists also weren't sure how long-term memories were formed in the brain. They now understand how the process happens, however, and why sleep is so important.

The Stages of Sleep

B What happens in the brain when we sleep? As the graph on the next page shows, the average adult goes through different sleep stages each night: REM (rapid eye movement) sleep, and three stages of non-REM sleep. When we first go to sleep, we proceed from REM sleep to Stage 1 of non-REM sleep, and then to Stages 2 and 3.

Non-REM Stage 3 is the deepest level of sleep. After that, we go back through the stages (Stage 3 → Stage 2 → Stage 1) and have a period of REM sleep before entering non-REM sleep again. We repeat this cycle four or five times each night. With each new cycle, the time spent in deep Stage 3 sleep decreases and the time spent in REM sleep increases.

Memory and the Brain

In 2009, a research team at Rutgers University discovered new information about the role of sleep in creating memories. The team found a type of brain activity that happens during sleep. The activity transfers new information from the

Stages and Cycles in Adult Sleep

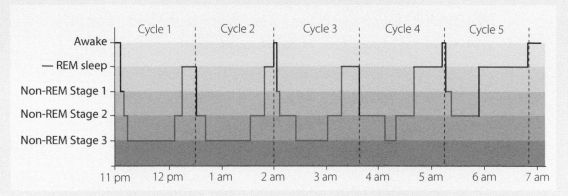

Source: http://www.howsleepworks.com

hippocampus to the neocortex—the part of the brain that stores long-term memories. The activity that occurs when information moves from the hippocampus to the neocortex looks like short, powerful waves. The Rutgers team called this brain activity "sharp wave ripples."[1] The brain creates these ripples in the hippocampus during the deepest level of sleep.

The Rutgers scientists discovered this wave activity in a study using rats. They trained the rats to learn a route in a maze. Then they let the rats sleep. They gave one group of sleeping rats a drug that stopped brain-wave activity. As a result, this group of rats had trouble remembering the route. The reason?

The new information was unable to leave the hippocampus and go to the neocortex.

Lifelong Memories

Because of the Rutgers study, we now know how the brain creates long-term memories. The study also proves that sleep is important for learning and memory. During deep sleep, brain-wave activity transfers short-term memories from the hippocampus to the neocortex. Then the sharp wave ripples "teach" the neocortex to make a long-term form of the memory. Researcher György Buzsáki says this is "why certain events may only take place once in the waking state and yet can be remembered for a lifetime."

TRAIN YOUR BRAIN!

Apart from getting enough sleep, there are other things you can do to improve your memory. Here are some tips:

- **Avoid stress.** Research shows that stress is bad for the brain. By avoiding stress, you may improve your memory. Physical exercise is one way to reduce stress.

- **Play games.** Some scientists say that mental activity might help memory. Puzzles, math problems, and even reading and writing can all benefit the brain.

- **Eat right.** Your brain can benefit from a healthy diet, just like the rest of your body. Foods that have antioxidants[2]—such as blueberries and spinach—are good for brain cells. This helps memory.

[1] A **ripple** is a slight movement of a surface (e.g., water).
[2] An **antioxidant** is a substance in food and other products that can prevent harmful chemical reactions from taking place in your body.

UNDERSTANDING THE READING

UNDERSTANDING
MAIN IDEAS

A Check (✓) the sentences that are supported by the reading passage.

☐ 1. The brain makes long-term memories while we sleep.

☐ 2. When we sleep, we go through cycles of sleep states.

☐ 3. Long-term memories are stored in the hippocampus.

☐ 4. During sleep, brain-wave activity connects the hippocampus with the neocortex.

☐ 5. One group of rats in the study couldn't remember the route because they got less sleep.

UNDERSTANDING A
PROCESS

B The flow chart below summarizes how the brain creates long-term memories. Complete the flow chart using information from the reading passage.

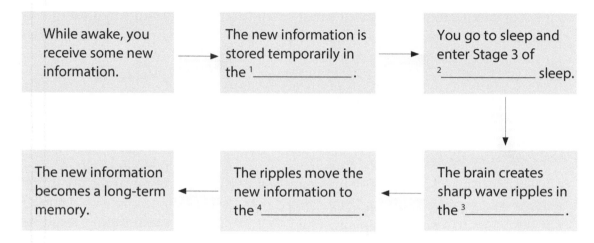

While awake, you receive some new information. → The new information is stored temporarily in the ¹_____. → You go to sleep and enter Stage 3 of ²_____ sleep.

The new information becomes a long-term memory. ← The ripples move the new information to the ⁴_____. ← The brain creates sharp wave ripples in the ³_____.

IDENTIFYING CAUSE
AND EFFECT

C Complete the chart below. Fill in the missing causes and effects.

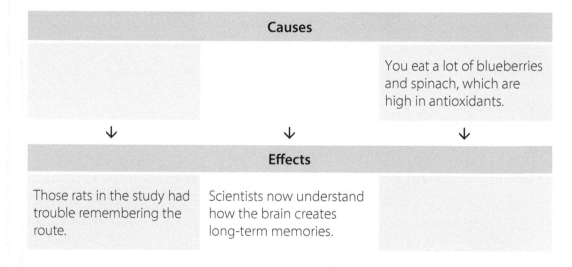

Causes		
		You eat a lot of blueberries and spinach, which are high in antioxidants.
↓	↓	↓

Effects		
Those rats in the study had trouble remembering the route.	Scientists now understand how the brain creates long-term memories.	

CRITICAL THINKING:
SYNTHESIZING

D List all the techniques and tips for improving memory that you have learned about in this unit. Circle the ones you are most likely to use.

_____

_____

Writing

EXPLORING WRITTEN ENGLISH

A Read the sentences below. Above each underlined portion, write **C** if it shows the cause or **E** if it shows the effect.

NOTICING

1. <u>By using the loci method</u>, Peter of Ravenna was able to "read" books stored in his memory palaces.

2. <u>You can memorize the colors of the rainbow in the order that they appear</u> by using the acronym ROY G BIV.

3. By learning "*i* before *e* except after *c* (where you hear *ee*)," <u>students of English can remember the spelling of words like *niece* and *receipt*</u>.

4. <u>Nelson Dellis set a record in the card event of the USA Memory Championship</u> by creating a coding system for his cards.

5. <u>By taking part in regular physical activity</u>, you can increase self-esteem and reduce stress.

6. By avoiding stress, <u>you may improve your memory</u>.

LANGUAGE FOR WRITING Using *By* + Gerund

There are many ways to show cause-and-effect relationships in your writing. One way to do this is with a *by* + gerund phrase. A gerund is a verb form that ends in *-ing*.

In a *by* + gerund phrase, you describe an activity that is the cause of something. The rest of the sentence expresses the result or effect. So, *by* + gerund expresses how to reach a result.

> **By exercising** *regularly, you can improve your memory.*
>   cause   effect

By + gerund phrases can appear at the beginning or at the end of a sentence. Use a comma when they appear at the beginning of a sentence.

> *You can improve your memory* **by getting** *enough sleep.*
> **By getting** *enough sleep, you can improve your memory.*

> *You can keep your brain healthy* **by eating** *foods that are high in antioxidants.*
> **By eating** *foods that are high in antioxidants, you can keep your brain healthy.*

B Combine the sentence parts using *by* + gerund.

Example: eat right / you can increase your brain power

By eating right, you can increase your brain power.

1. get a good night's sleep / you help your brain form long-term memories

   _____

   _____

2. you can memorize the order of a deck of cards / use the loci method

   _____

   _____

3. the scientists stopped the rats' brain waves / give them a drug

   _____

   _____

4. make a shopping list / you can remember what items you need to buy

   _____

   _____

C Write three sentences using the *by* + gerund form. Describe ways you relieve stress and ways you can improve your diet.

1. _____

2. _____

3. _____

WRITING SKILL Using an Outline

Using an outline helps you to organize and develop your ideas before you write. A good outline is like a map: It gives you something to follow while you write.

To write an outline for a paragraph, first think about the topic and list a few supporting ideas. Then write a topic sentence that introduces your supporting ideas. The topic sentence should clearly state the main idea of the paragraph. Finally, write down details that explain each supporting idea. The details might be examples, a list of reasons, or steps in a process. Apart from the topic sentence, don't write complete sentences in an outline.

By following an outline, you improve the flow of your writing. It also helps you make sure that you don't miss any important points or include any unrelated information.

D Look at the outline below and read the paragraph that follows. Match the sentences in the paragraph (a–j) to the parts of the outline. Three sentences are extra.

OUTLINE

Topic: How to Memorize a Route

Topic Sentence:	_____
Supporting Idea 1: memorize as steps	_____
Details: write names, directions	_____
read and repeat	_____
Supporting Idea 2: create mental picture	_____
Details: study a map	_____
imagine following route	_____

a. When you have to memorize a route, you should use a technique that works well for you. **b.** Many people use driving apps nowadays, so they don't need to memorize a route. **c.** One technique is to memorize directions as a set of steps. **d.** To do this, write the street names and directions in the correct order on a piece of paper. For example, Step 1 might be: "Drive three miles down Main Street." Step 2 might be: "Turn right on Oak Street." **e.** Read what you have written several times. After a while, you won't have to look at the paper anymore. **f.** You can also memorize a route by creating a mental picture of it. **g.** That is, you can form an image of the streets and the places on the streets in your mind. **h.** To do this, study the route as it appears on a map. **i.** Then close your eyes and imagine yourself following the route. Turn your body to the right and to the left as you make the turns and pass the buildings. By visualizing the route, you will learn it faster. **j.** There are other ways to learn routes; use the method that works best for you.

E Look again at the three sentences that didn't match the outline. Match each sentence to a description.

_____ provides an explanation of a key concept

_____ provides a concluding statement

_____ is not relevant to the main idea of the paragraph

F Look back at sentences a–j in exercise D. Find and underline three cause-effect relationships.

WRITING TASK

GOAL You are going to write a paragraph on the following topic:
What can a person do to improve their memory?

BRAINSTORMING **A** Look back at your list for exercise D on page 14. Work with a partner. Can you think of any other ways a person could improve their memory? Add ideas to your list.

_____

_____

PLANNING **B** Follow these steps to complete an outline for your paragraph.

Step 1 From your notes above and on page 14, choose your best two or three techniques and note them as your supporting ideas in the outline below.

Step 2 Write a topic sentence that introduces your supporting ideas.

Step 3 Now write two details or examples for each supporting idea. Don't worry about grammar or spelling. Don't write complete sentences.

OUTLINE

Topic: How to Improve Your Memory

Topic Sentence: _____

_____

Supporting Idea 1: _____

Details: _____

_____

Supporting Idea 2: _____

Details: _____

_____

Supporting Idea 3: _____

Details: _____

_____

FIRST DRAFT **C** Use the information in your outline to write a first draft of your paragraph.

REVISING PRACTICE

The drafts below are similar to the one you are going to write. They are on the topic of how people can keep lasting memories.

What did the writer do in Draft 2 to improve the paragraph? Match the changes (a–d) to the highlighted parts. Some can be used more than once.

a. added a detail to a supporting idea
b. made the topic sentence stronger
c. corrected a verb form
d. deleted unrelated information

Draft 1

You can record the important events in life so that they will become lasting memories. One way is to keep a written journal. This is a written record of events, activities, and thoughts. You can also include photos in your journal. Another way to create lasting memories is to keep a video journal. With a video journal, you can record activities and events as they are happening. You can also make recordings afterwards of yourself talking about the events or activities. My phone has a video recorder, but sometimes it doesn't work very well. By use these methods, you can create lasting memories that you will enjoy for many years.

Draft 2

There are two main ways to record the important events in life so that they will become lasting memories. One way is to keep a written journal. This is a written record of events, activities, and thoughts. You can write it by hand in a notebook, or type it on a computer. You can also include photos in your journal. Label each one by date, place, and the names of the people in the photos so that you'll be able to remember them later. Another way to create lasting memories is to keep a video journal. With a video journal, you can record activities and events as they are happening. You can also make recordings afterwards of yourself talking about the events or activities. By using these methods, you can create lasting memories that you will enjoy for many years.

D Now use the questions below to revise your paragraph.

REVISED DRAFT

- [ ] Does a strong topic sentence introduce the main idea?
- [ ] Are there two or three different supporting ideas?
- [ ] Are there at least two details or examples for each supporting idea?
- [ ] Are all verb forms correct?
- [ ] Is there any information that doesn't belong?
- [ ] Is there a concluding sentence?

EDITING PRACTICE

Read the information below.

In cause-and-effect sentences using a *by* + gerund phrase, remember to:
- use the *-ing* form of the verb.
- use a comma when the *by* + gerund phrase appears at the beginning of a sentence.

Correct one *by* + gerund mistake in each sentence below.

1. You can't remember all of the information in a lecture just by listen to it.

2. By taking notes while you listen you can remember information better.

3. By write a summary of your notes after a lecture, you will remember the information more easily.

4. By taking notes and make lists, you transfer information from internal to external memory.

5. One study shows that by getting a good night's sleep people remember a skill (such as playing the piano) 30 percent better.

6. You can improve your memory by eating a healthy diet and exercise regularly.

FINAL DRAFT   **E**   **Follow these steps to write a final draft.**

1. Check your revised draft for mistakes with the *by* + gerund form.

2. Now use the checklist on page 79 to write a final draft. Make any other necessary changes.

UNIT REVIEW

Answer the following questions.

1. In your opinion, which memorization technique mentioned in this unit is most effective?

_____

_____

2. Why do writers use the *by* + gerund phrase in sentences?

_____

_____

3. Do you remember the meanings of these words? Check (✓) the ones you know. Look back at the unit and review the ones you don't know.

Reading 1:

☐ achievement AWL   ☐ complex AWL   ☐ external AWL
☐ familiar   ☐ gradually   ☐ internal AWL
☐ memorize   ☐ technique AWL   ☐ text AWL
☐ visualize AWL

Reading 2:

☐ drug   ☐ mental AWL   ☐ physical AWL
☐ proof   ☐ route AWL   ☐ state
☐ stress AWL   ☐ transfer AWL

Answer to **Before Viewing** A-1, page 9: 16.96 seconds (set in 2016 by Alex Mullen)

NOTES

NOTES

A Compact Muon Solenoid, a particle physics detector, looks for the Higgs boson particle.

ME+4/1/03

ME+4/1/02

ME+4/1/01

ME+4/1/18

ME+4/1/17

E+4/1/16

*Can you write the steps
in a process for doing
something?*

What Is a Process Paragraph?

At times, you are required to describe how to do something or how something works. In a process paragraph, you divide a process into separate steps. You list or explain the steps in chronological order—the order of events as they happen over time. Special time words or phrases allow you to tell the reader the sequence of the steps. The process paragraph ends with a specific result—something that happens at the end of the process.

A process paragraph:

- explains a sequence or process
- presents facts and details in chronological order
- uses time words or phrases
- ends with a specified result

ACTIVITY 1 Studying Example Process Paragraphs

The three paragraphs that follow are about different topics, and each one is an example of a process paragraph. Discuss the Preview Questions with your classmates. Then read the example paragraphs and answer the questions that follow.

Process Paragraph 1

The topic of this paragraph is a popular Mexican dish. People have to be careful when they eat this food because it can be messy.

Preview Questions

1. Do you know any Mexican food dishes? Do you know the ingredients? If so, what are they?

2. Are any of these dishes messy when you eat them? If so, what makes them messy?

3. Name a food that you have eaten that was very messy. How did you eat it?

Example Paragraph 1

Eating a <u>Messy</u> Food

Because eating a delicious, juicy **taco** is not easy, it requires following specific directions. First, you must be sure that you are wearing clothes that you do not mind getting dirty. Eating a taco while you are wearing an expensive shirt or suit is not a smart idea. The next thing that you should do is decide if you want to eat the taco alone or in front of others. Eating a taco in front of someone you do not know well can be **embarrassing**. Finally, it is important to plan your attack! It is a good idea to pick up the taco gently and then carefully keep it in a **horizontal** position. As you raise the taco, slowly turn your head toward it and position your head at a 20-degree **angle**. The last step is to put the corner of the taco in your mouth and take a bite. By following these simple directions, eating a taco can be a less messy experience.

messy: not neat

a taco: a Mexican dish consisting of a tortilla wrapped around a mixture of meat, lettuce, tomato, cheese, and sauce

embarrassing: causing a self-conscious or uncomfortable feeling

horizontal: across, from side to side (opposite of vertical)

an angle: where two lines meet

Post-Reading

1. What is the topic sentence of this paragraph?

   _____

   _____

2. This paragraph discusses three directions for eating tacos. What are they?

   a. _Do not wear expensive clothes because you might spill something on them._

   _____

   b. _____

   _____

   c. _____

   _____

3. Do you think that the writer's tone in this paragraph is serious, angry, or humorous?

   _____ Why? _____

   _____

4. Is there any information that you would like to add?

   _____

   _____

Process Paragraph 2

1. What is your favorite strategy for increasing your English vocabulary?

2. Do you keep a vocabulary notebook or written record of new English vocabulary? Why do you do this? (OR Why don't you do this?)

Example Paragraph 2

Keeping a Vocabulary Notebook

Keeping a vocabulary notebook for learning new English words is not complicated if you follow a few easy steps. First, you must buy a notebook with at least 100 lined pages. You should select the color and size notebook that you prefer. Second, you have to write down any important words that you find when reading or listening. This step requires you to decide whether a word is important enough for you to

try to learn it by including it in your vocabulary list. Do not assume that you will remember the word later. The next step is a bit difficult because you need to decide what information about each word you will write down in your notebook. Some learners write only a translation of the word. Other people write an example phrase using the word. Some people write a synonym in English. Of course you can write all three pieces of information. When you are trying to decide what to write, you should remember that this notebook is yours, and you should include information that will help you remember the word. You can include information that matches your personality and your needs. Finally, the most important thing you can do to learn the words in your notebook is to practice these words several times. If the pages of your notebook are neat and inviting, you are more likely to review the words and their information multiple times. If you follow these important steps in keeping a good vocabulary notebook, you can improve your English greatly.

1. What is the topic sentence of the paragraph?

_____

_____

2. How many steps does the author give? _____

3. Does the paragraph explain the difference between vocabulary you find in reading and the vocabulary you find in speaking? _____ Why or why not?

_____

4. What are the "three pieces of information" mentioned in the paragraph?

_____

_____

_____

Process Paragraph 3

Preview Questions

1. Describe a magic trick that you saw someone do. Who was it? What did the person do? Do you know the secret of that trick?

2. Can you do a magic trick? If so, describe the trick.

Guessing Your Friend's Number

I am going to explain the steps to do a really interesting math trick that I learned yesterday that will amaze your friends. First, tell your friends that their answer will be three **no matter** what they do. Now tell your friends to think of a number **greater** than zero. Third, they should multiply their number by itself. Next, they should add their answer to their original number. Now they should divide their new total by their original number. In the sixth step, your friends should add 17 and then subtract their original answer from this last total. Finally, they should divide their answer by six. The final result is always three. Your friends will think you have the ability to know what they are thinking, but you know this is a simple math trick where the answer is always three.

no matter: it does not make any difference

greater: larger, bigger

1. List the first three steps in this math trick.

   _____

   _____

   _____

2. This process has many small steps. Good writers do not always write one sentence for each small step. Instead, they combine some steps in longer sentences. Write a sentence from this paragraph that has more than one step in it.

   _____

   _____

3. For additional practice, choose two steps and combine them in one sentence. Compare your sentence with a classmate.

   _____

   _____

Grammar for Writing

Using Sequence Words and Chronological Order

The three paragraphs in Activity 1 each describe how to do or make something. The writers use chronological order to show the reader when the steps in the process occur.

To show time order in a process, writers use **time phrases, time clauses,** and **time words** such as *first, second, then, next, the next step, the last thing…, in addition, before,* and *after.* These items are also called **sequence words** or **transition words** because they mark the transition from one step to the next.

Sequence Words	Examples from Activity 1
First, (Second, Third, etc.)	**First,** you must buy a notebook with at least 100 pages.
The next thing / step	**The next thing** that you should do is decide if you want to eat the taco alone or in front of others.
Next,	**Next,** they should add their answer to their original number.
The last step	**The last step** is to put the corner of the taco in your mouth and take a bite.
Finally,	**Finally,** they should divide their answer by six.

Writer's Note

Using Notecards to Help You Organize

It is important that all the steps in your process paragraph be in the correct order. A simple way for you to organize the steps is to write each one on a small card. This organization method will allow you to arrange and rearrange the steps. It will also help point out any steps that may be missing.

ACTIVITY 2 Sequencing Sentences

The following sentences about tennis make up a paragraph. Number them from 1 to 8 to indicate the best order. Then underline all the words or phrases that show time order or sequence. (If you are not familiar with tennis, ask a person who plays tennis to explain how to serve or watch a video clip of a tennis player serving.)

_____ **a.** Hit the ball into the small box on the opposite side of the net.

_____ **b.** After you hit the ball, continue swinging your racket down and across the front of your body.

_____ **c.** Just before the ball reaches its peak, begin to swing your racket forward as high as you can reach.

_____ **d.** First, toss the ball with your left hand about three feet in the air. The best position for the ball is just to the right of your head.

_____ **e.** At the same time, move your racket behind your shoulder with your right hand so that your elbow is pointed toward the sky.

_____ **f.** After you have completed the serve, your racket should be near your left knee.

_____ **g.** Many people think serving in tennis is difficult, but the following steps show that it is quite easy.

_____ **h.** If you are left-handed, you should substitute the words _left_ and _right_ in the preceding directions.

ACTIVITY 3 **Sequencing Information in Paragraph Form**

Copy the sentences from Activity 2 in paragraph form. The result will be a process paragraph. Give the paragraph an original title.

Example Paragraph 4

_____

_____

_____

_____

_____

_____

_____

_____

_____

_____

_____

_____

ACTIVITY 4 **Analyzing and Understanding a Paragraph**

Read Example Paragraph 4 in Activity 3 again or refer to it as you complete the answers to these questions.

1. What is the general topic of the paragraph?

_____

2. What is the topic sentence?

_____

_____

3. The main purpose of this paragraph is to explain how to serve a tennis ball. However, the author also expresses an opinion in the topic sentence. Read the topic sentence again. What is that opinion?

_____

_____

4. Look at this sentence from the paragraph: "The best position for the ball is just to the right of your head." Unlike the other sentences, this is not a step. What is the purpose of this sentence?

_____

_____

_____

_____

ACTIVITY 5 **Using Commas and Sequence Expressions**

Transitional words, phrases, and clauses can show chronological order. Most transitional words and clauses are followed by a comma. The following sentences make up a paragraph. Number them from 1 to 10 to indicate the best order. Then, add commas where necessary. Hint: Five sentences need commas.

_____ **a.** First put the water and the plants in the jar.

_____ **b.** One week later check the fish.

_____ **c.** The fact that the fish is still alive shows that oxygen was added. If you look carefully at a plant stem when it is in sunlight, you can see the tiny bubbles of oxygen escaping from the plant.

_____ **d.** When you do this be sure to leave about an inch of empty space.

_____ **e.** Keep the jar in a cool place indoors, but be sure that it receives some direct sunlight for a few hours each day.

_____ **f.** When you are sure that the water in the jar is at room temperature add the fish.

_____ **g.** Here is a simple science experiment that proves that plants produce oxygen.

_____ **h.** For this experiment, you will need a clean quart jar with a tight lid, some tape, a goldfish, some water, and a few green plants.

_____ **i.** Put the lid on as tightly as you can.

_____ **j.** After that wrap the lid with several layers of tape so that you are sure that no air can pass through it.

ACTIVITY 6 Writing a Paragraph with Sequence Expressions

The sentences in Activity 5 explain the steps of a simple science experiment. After you have added commas and arranged the sentences in the correct order, write the completed process paragraph on the lines below. Create a title for the paragraph.

Example Paragraph 5

_____

_____

_____

_____

_____

_____

_____

_____

_____

_____

_____

_____

_____

_____

_____

_____

Building Better Vocabulary

ACTIVITY 7 **Word Associations**

Circle the word or phrase that is most closely related to the word or phrase on the left. If necessary, use a dictionary to check the meaning of words you do not know.

	A	B
1. the peak	the lowest point	the highest point
2. a phrase	right here	We are right here.
3. preceding	before	after
4. a synonym	different	similar
5. to prove	to show	to try
6. horizontal	left ⟺ right	up ⇕ down
7. messy	not neat	not original
8. quite	silent	very
9. a jar	made of glass	made of paper
10. your knee	arm	leg
11. amaze	believe	surprise
12. to remind	to release	to remember
13. your shoulder	body	mind
14. a stem	an animal	a plant

ACTIVITY 8 Using Collocations

Fill in each blank with the word on the left that most naturally completes the phrase on the right. If necessary, use a dictionary to check the meaning of words you do not know.

1. get / put   to _____ ready

2. make / take   _____ a bite

3. down / up   pick _____

4. the Internet / a problem   to point out _____

5. elbow / remind   my left _____

6. from / than   greater _____

7. for / of   he reminded me _____ my father

8. comma / side   the opposite _____

9. tape / tiny   _____ bubbles

10. from / than   greater _____ zero

11. lid / plant   a tight _____

12. direct / empty   an inch of _____ space

Original Student Writing: Process Paragraph

ACTIVITY 9 Original Writing Practice

Write a process paragraph. Follow these guidelines:

- Choose a topic about something you know how to do or you know how it is done, or look at the opening photograph for an idea.

- Write some notes about the steps in the process.

- Write a topic sentence with one or more controlling ideas.

- Write supporting sentences that give the steps in chronological order. Use transition words to show that the steps are in the correct order.

- Use at least two of the vocabulary words or phrases presented in Activity 7 and Activity 8. Underline these words and phrases in your paragraph.

- If you need help, study the example process paragraphs in this unit. Be sure to refer to the seven steps in the writing process in the *Brief Writer's Handbook*, pages 80–86.

If you need ideas for words and phrases, see the Useful Vocabulary for Better Writing on pages 109–113.

ACTIVITY 10 Peer Editing

Exchange papers from Activity 9 with a partner. Read your partner's paragraph. Then use Peer Editing Sheet 1 on ELTNGL.com/sites/els to help you comment on your partner's paragraph. Be sure to offer positive suggestions and comments that will help your partner improve his or her writing. Consider your partner's comments as you revise your own paragraph.

Additional Topics for Writing

Here are some ideas for process paragraphs. When you write your paragraph, follow the guidelines in Activity 9.

PHOTO
TOPIC: Write about a process or how something happens, for example a scientific experiment or a weather phenomenon, such as lightning, fog, a tornado, or a hurricane.

TOPIC 2: Write about the steps in writing a good paragraph. How do you start? What information do you include?

TOPIC 3: Write about the steps a successful job applicant should follow. Where do you start? What resources do you use?

TOPIC 4: Write about what you need to do to get a driver's license.

TOPIC 5: Describe how to use the Internet to find the very best price for something.

Timed Writing

How quickly can you write in English? There are many times when you must write quickly, such as on a test. It is important to feel comfortable during those times. Timed-writing practice can make you feel better about writing quickly in English.

1. Take out a piece of paper.

2. Read the writing prompt.

3. Brainstorm ideas for five minutes.

4. Write a short paragraph (six to ten sentences).

5. You have 25 minutes to write.

From time to time, a bank or other business sends a bill or statement that has a mistake. (For example, a credit card bill may have charged you twice for a certain item.) What are the steps in correcting an error on a bill?

Or

What should you do if the server at a restaurant has given you your bill with an error on it? How can you rectify this situation?

NOTES

NATURE'S FURY

3

Lightning strikes over the town of Barr, France.

THINK AND DISCUSS

1 What types of extreme natural events can you think of?
2 Which of these natural events are the most dangerous? Why?

A Look at the information on these pages and answer the questions.

1. Which events have natural causes? Which event is normally caused by human activity?

2. Which event can cause another to start? Which event can create its own weather system?

B Match the correct form of the words in blue to their definitions.

_____ (v) to happen

_____ (v) to hit something suddenly

_____ (adj) very strong or powerful

Lightning, tornadoes, and wildfires all cause destruction. **Lightning** strikes somewhere on Earth about 100 times every second. It's extremely hot—it can heat the air around it to temperatures five times hotter than the surface of the sun. In most cases, lightning is caused by electrical activity in clouds.

Tornadoes, also called twisters, are born from thunderstorms. They occur when warm, moist (wet) air meets cold, dry air. Moving at up to 250 mph (400 kph), tornadoes are the fastest winds on Earth. They can form at any time of the day, but they happen most often in the late afternoon, when large thunderstorms are common.

Wildfires move at speeds of up to 14 mph (23 kph). Four out of five wildfires are caused by human activity. A natural event such as lightning can also start a wildfire. A large, **violent** wildfire can create its own weather system: Air around the fire gets warmer, the warm air rises, and this process sometimes creates winds.

EXTREME NATURE

A tornado develops from a thunderstorm over farmland in Colorado.

A firefighter tackles a wildfire near San Andreas, California.

CONFLICTING THEORIES

D

What caused the outbreak of violent tornadoes in 2011? Experts aren't sure. Some think warmer-than-normal water temperatures in the Gulf of Mexico—a result of global warming—were the cause. Russell Schneider, director of the U.S. Storm Prediction Center, thinks the outbreak occurred largely because of a weather pattern called "La Niña." La Niña occurs when cold water in the Pacific Ocean rises to the surface off the coast of South America. This can also affect the climate in the United States and create more thunderstorms and tornadoes.

E

Pablo Saide, a scientist at the University of Iowa, has another theory. He believes that fires in Central America may be part of the cause. These fires are set every year to clear land for farming. Smoke drifting[2] into the United States raises air temperature, which can lead to cloud formation and irregular wind patterns—common risk factors for tornadoes. "We're not saying that the outbreak happened because of the smoke," says Saide. "We're saying that, given the conditions already in place, the smoke intensified the tornadoes."

F

Scientists around the world continue to gather data about tornadoes. One day, their research will help us to better understand the conditions that cause violent tornadoes to form. Eventually, we may be able to predict how strong they will be and where they will hit, and take preventive measures to minimize loss of life.

▼ Tornadoes may occur wherever warm, moist air collides with cool, dry air.

[2]When something drifts somewhere, it is carried there by the movement of wind or water.

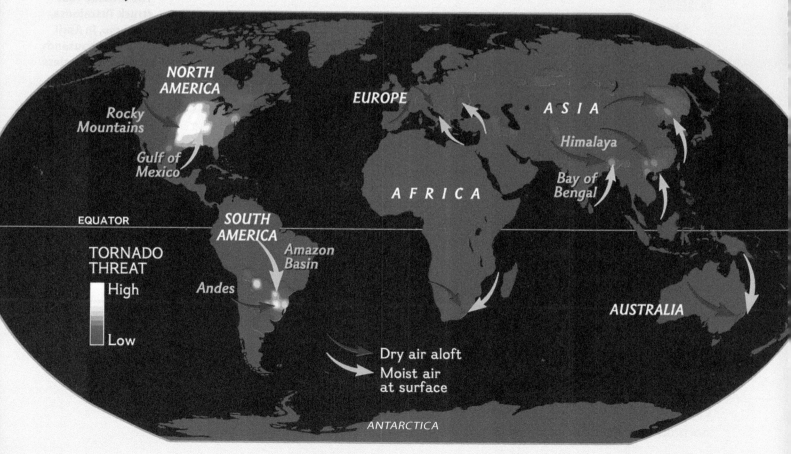

UNDERSTANDING THE READING

A Match each section from the reading passage (1–4) to its purpose.

UNDERSTANDING
MAIN IDEAS

_____ 1. Paragraph A   a. to highlight an area where tornadoes usually occur
_____ 2. Paragraph B   b. to give possible reasons for the violent tornadoes
_____ 3. Paragraph C   c. to explain what was unusual about the Tuscaloosa tornado
_____ 4. Paragraphs D–E   d. to provide some facts about the April 2011 tornado season

B What may have caused the violent tornadoes in April 2011? Fill in the missing information in the flow chart below.

UNDERSTANDING
CAUSE AND EFFECT

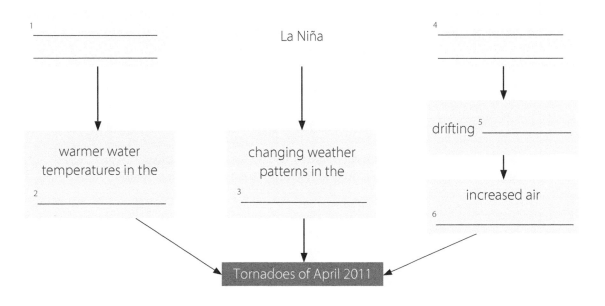

1 _____

La Niña

4 _____

warmer water temperatures in the
2 _____

changing weather patterns in the
3 _____

drifting 5 _____

increased air
6 _____

Tornadoes of April 2011

CRITICAL THINKING   To find out whether or not a **source** is credible, you **evaluate** it. What are the source's credentials? Consider the source's professional or educational background, experience, and past writing.

C Read the following excerpts from the reading passage. Then discuss the questions with a partner.

CRITICAL THINKING:
EVALUATING
SOURCES

"There were no limitations," said tornado expert and storm chaser Tim Samaras. "It went absolutely crazy. It had nothing but hundreds of miles to grow and develop."

Russell Schneider, director of the U.S. Storm Prediction Center, thinks the outbreak occurred largely because of a weather pattern called "La Niña."

Pablo Saide, a scientist at the University of Iowa, has another theory. He believes that fires in Central America may be part of the cause.

1. How does the writer describe Samaras, Schneider, and Saide? For which source(s) do you have more specific information?

2. Do you find each of these sources credible? Why or why not?

D Look at the map on page 44. Apart from North America, where else do tornadoes strike? Discuss with a partner.

INTERPRETING
MAPS

DEVELOPING READING SKILLS

UNDERSTANDING
A PROCESS

A The illustration below shows how twisters form. Read the captions. Complete the missing information using the words in the box. One word is used twice.

| air | cold | ground | spin | warm |

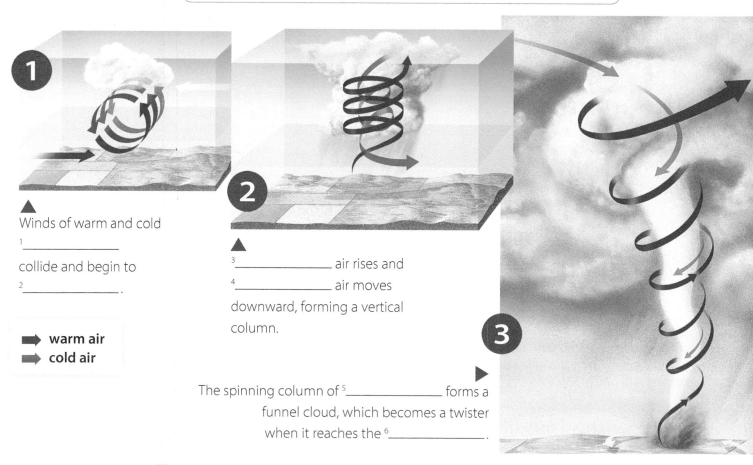

▲ Winds of warm and cold
¹_____ collide and begin to
²_____ .

➡ warm air
➡ cold air

▲ ³_____ air rises and
⁴_____ air moves downward, forming a vertical column.

▶ The spinning column of ⁵_____ forms a funnel cloud, which becomes a twister when it reaches the ⁶_____ .

IDENTIFYING
SEQUENCE

B Now write a paragraph about how twisters form based on the captions in exercise A. Use sequencing words in your paragraph.

LIGHTNING

A lightning storm lights up the sky over a desert.

BEFORE VIEWING

A Read the sentences and guess if they are correct. Circle **T** for true or **F** for false. You will learn the answers while watching the video.

PREDICTING

1. Lightning is electricity.   T   F

2. Lightning occurs about 1,000 times a second worldwide.   T   F

3. Lightning strikes are more common in Europe than in South America.   T   F

4. On average, more people in the United States are killed by lightning than by tornadoes.   T   F

B Read the information about lightning. Then answer the questions.

LEARNING ABOUT THE TOPIC

Lightning is extremely hot. A bolt of lightning can raise air temperature by as much as 50,000 degrees Fahrenheit (27,700 degrees Celsius); that's five times hotter than the surface of the sun. When lightning strikes sand, it can melt it, creating a tube-shaped rock called a fulgurite. Lightning can even kill people. The average American has about a 1 in 5,000 chance of being struck by lightning during their lifetime. In the United States, most lightning happens during the summer months. The Fourth of July is historically one of the deadliest times of year for lightning in the country.

1. What can happen to sand when lightning hits it?

   _____

2. Why do you think the Fourth of July is such a dangerous time for lightning strikes?

   _____

C The words in **bold** below are used in the video. Match the correct form of each word to its definition.

> When tiny **particles** of ice collide within thunderclouds, the contact creates an electrical **charge**.
>
> A fully charged car battery should measure at 12.6 **volts** or above.
>
> Lightning strikes can cause forest fires; when drought conditions exist in the forest, fires often **expand** quickly.

1. _____ (v) to get bigger

2. _____ (n) a unit used to measure the force of an electric current

3. _____ (n) a very small piece of matter

4. _____ (n) the type of electricity that something contains (existing in a positive or negative form)

WHILE VIEWING

A ▶ Watch the video. Check (✓) the topics that are discussed.

☐ 1. where in the world lightning frequently occurs

☐ 2. how lightning is formed

☐ 3. warning signs of lightning and thunderstorms

☐ 4. what to do if you are caught in a thunderstorm

☐ 5. how to protect your home from lightning

B ▶ Watch the video again. Circle the correct words.

1. Regions that have the most lightning strikes include Central Africa, the Himalayas, and **Europe** / **South America**.

2. In a storm cloud, lighter particles become **positively** / **negatively** charged, while heavier particles become **positively** / **negatively** charged.

3. The sound of thunder is caused by the **expanding air** / **electrical charges** around the lightning.

4. During a lightning storm, you can stay safe by **getting in a car** / **standing under a tree**.

AFTER VIEWING

A Check your answers to exercise A of **Before Viewing**. Were your predictions correct? Did any information from the video surprise you?

B Look back at the map on page 44. Discuss these questions with a partner.

1. Where in the world do both tornadoes and frequent lightning occur?

2. Based on what you have learned in this unit, where are the safest regions in the world to live?

Reading 2

PREPARING TO READ

A The words and phrases in blue below are used in the reading passage on pages 50–51. Read their definitions and then complete each sentence with the correct form of the word or phrase.

> If something is **appropriate**, it is suitable for a particular situation.
>
> To **block** something means to make its movement difficult or impossible.
>
> If something is **frequent**, it happens often.
>
> **Fuel** is a material (such as coal, wood, oil, or gas) that is burned to produce heat or power.
>
> If you do something **on purpose**, you do it intentionally.
>
> **Particularly** means more than usual or more than other things.
>
> If something is described as **significant**, it is large enough to be noticeable.
>
> Something that **threatens** a person or thing is likely to cause harm.

1. _____ lightning storms are dangerous. Many storms in a short period of time can cause fires that _____ people's lives.

2. Fires that occur in places where a lot of people live are _____ dangerous.

3. Many fires are the result of accidents. However, firefighters sometimes set small, controlled fires _____ to prevent larger fires later on.

4. Different types of fire extinguishers are designed to fight different types of fire. To successfully put out a fire, you must use the _____ extinguisher.

5. Corridors and stairwells should be kept clear of any objects that might _____ people's exit during a fire.

6. In 2016, a series of wildfires burned across the state of California, consuming all the _____ in their path—such as trees, grass, and homes—and causing _____ damage.

B Discuss these questions with a partner.

1. Do fires occur **frequently** in your community? Why or why not?
2. If there is a fire in a crowded building, what is the **appropriate** thing to do?

C Look at the illustration on pages 50–51. What do you think the reading passage is mainly about? Check your answer as you read.

a. the main causes or sources of wildfires
b. how to prevent wildfires from spreading
c. the effect of wildfires on the environment

WILDFIRES!

A   Wildfires occur all around the world, but they are most frequent in areas that have wet seasons followed by long, hot, dry seasons. These conditions exist in parts of Australia, South Africa, southern Europe, and the western regions of the United States. These places therefore experience particularly dangerous fires.

B   A wildfire can move quickly and destroy large areas of land in just a few minutes. There are three conditions that need to be present in order for a fire to burn: fuel, oxygen, and a heat source. Fuel can be anything in the path of the fire that can burn—trees, grass, and even homes. Air supplies the oxygen. Heat sources include lightning, hot winds—like the Santa Ana winds in California—and even heat from the sun. However, most wildfires are caused by people, not nature, especially from cigarettes and campfires.

C   When trying to put out a fire, firefighters must consider three main factors: the shape of the land, the weather, and the type of fuel in the path of the fire. For example, fire often moves faster uphill. Southern sides of mountains are sunnier and drier, so they are more likely to burn than the northern sides. Also, strong winds can suddenly change the direction of a fire. This could put firefighters directly in the fire's path and threaten their safety. Sudden changes in wind direction also make it hard to predict the spread of a fire. Lastly, dry grass and dead trees tend to burn faster than trees with lots of moisture.

D   From past experience, we know that it is difficult to prevent wildfires, but it is possible to stop them from becoming too big. One strategy is to cut down trees. Another is to start fires on purpose to clear land. Both of these strategies limit the amount of fuel available for fires by removing plants and trees. In addition, people who live in areas where wildfires frequently occur can build fire-resistant[1] homes, says fire researcher Jack Cohen. Cohen has studied wildfires for more than two decades and is an expert on how houses catch fire. "In California there were significant cases of communities that did not burn," he says, "because they were fire-resistant."

E   Most experts agree that no single action will solve the wildfire problem entirely. The best method is to consider all these strategies and use each of them when and where they are the most appropriate.

[1]If something is fire-resistant, it does not catch fire easily.

FIGHTING FIRE

- To control a wildfire, firefighters on the ground first look for something in the area that can **block** the fire, such as a river or a road. Then they dig a deep trench[2] along it. This is a "fire line"—a line that fire cannot cross. **1**

- While firefighters on the ground create a fire line, planes and helicopters drop water or chemical fire retardant[3] on the fire. **2** Pilots communicate with firefighters on the ground so they know which areas to hit.

- After the fire line is created, firefighters cut down any dead trees in the area between the fire line and the fire. **3** This helps keep flames from climbing higher into the treetops.

- At the same time, other firefighters on the ground begin backburning[4] in the area between the fire line and the fire. **4**

[2]A **trench** is a long, narrow hole that is dug in the ground.
[3]**Fire retardant** is a type of chemical that slows the burning of fire.
[4]**Backburning** involves removing fuel (such as plants and trees) in a fire's path by burning it in a controlled way.

UNDERSTANDING THE READING

UNDERSTANDING
MAIN IDEAS

A Match each paragraph from the reading passage to its purpose.

_____ 1. Paragraph A   a. to describe the necessary conditions for a fire
_____ 2. Paragraph B   b. to explain how to protect ourselves from wildfires
_____ 3. Paragraph C   c. to highlight areas where wildfires are most common
_____ 4. Paragraph D   d. to describe what firefighters should look out for in a fire

UNDERSTANDING
DETAILS

B What are the main factors that firefighters consider when they are trying to put out a fire? What are examples of each one? Complete the chart using information from the reading passage.

Factor	Shape of the land		
Examples			dry grass, dead trees

UNDERSTANDING
A PROCESS

C How do firefighters control a wildfire? Read the sentences. Circle **T** for true or **F** for false.

1. Firefighters dig a trench to create a fire line. **T** **F**

2. Planes and helicopters drop fire retardant on the fire line. **T** **F**

3. Firefighters cut down dead trees in the area to control the fire. **T** **F**

4. Firefighters backburn the area behind the fire line, far away from the oncoming fire. **T** **F**

CRITICAL THINKING:
EVALUATING SOURCES

D Discuss these questions with a partner.

1. Who is Jack Cohen? How does the writer describe him?

2. What idea does Cohen's quote support?

3. On a scale from 1 to 3, how credible a source do you think Cohen is? (1 = not credible; 3 = very credible) Share your rating with a partner and discuss your reasons.

4. What other information about Cohen could the writer have provided?

CRITICAL THINKING:
EVALUATING SOURCES

E If you were writing this passage, who would you include as an additional source? Circle your answer and note your reasons. Then share your decision with a partner.

a. a wildland firefighter who has just completed basic training
b. an experienced pilot of a firefighting plane
c. a scientist who has studied fire ecology for 30 years
d. an owner of a fire-resistant home

Reason(s): _____

_____

Writing

EXPLORING WRITTEN ENGLISH

A The sentences below describe the rainwater cycle. Read each sentence and underline NOTICING the verb(s).

1. The sun raises the temperature of water in rivers, lakes, and oceans.

2. When the water heats up, some of it turns into vapor or steam.

3. The vapor rises into the air.

4. As the vapor rises, it gets cold and turns into tiny water droplets that form clouds in the sky.

5. The clouds get heavy, and water falls back to Earth in the form of rain.

6. The cycle continues.

What tense are the underlined verbs? _____

LANGUAGE FOR WRITING Describing a Process

Writers usually use the simple present tense to describe a natural or biological process—that is, to explain how something happens. For example:

*Warm air **moves** upward.*

*When vapor in the air **gets** cold enough, it **changes** back into tiny water droplets.*

*These water droplets **combine** with dust particles in the air and **form** visible clouds.*

*Within a thundercloud, tiny particles of ice **bump** into each other as they **move** around in the air.*

*All of these collisions **create** an electrical charge.*

*After a while, the whole cloud **fills** up with electrical charges.*

Remember to make subjects and verbs agree when you use the simple present tense.

B The following sentences describe how snow is formed. Complete the sentences using the correct form of the verbs in parentheses.

1. When the temperature in the clouds _____ (*be*) very low, the vapor in the air _____ (*freeze*) and _____ (*turn*) into tiny ice crystals.

2. When the tiny ice crystals _____ (*collide*), they _____ (*stick*) together in clouds and _____ (*form*) snowflakes.

3. Each snowflake _____ (*start*) out very small and then _____ (*grow*) bigger.

4. When the snowflakes _____ (become) too heavy, they _____ (fall) to the ground.

5. After snow _____ (fall) to the ground, it either _____ (melt) or _____ (stay) frozen, depending on the land surface temperature.

C In your own words, write three sentences in the simple present tense about how tornadoes, lightning, and/or wildfires form.

1. _____

_____

2. _____

_____

3. _____

_____

WRITING SKILL Organizing a Process Paragraph

When you write a process paragraph, you explain steps or events in **chronological order**—the first event appears first, then the next event, and so on.

To plan a process paragraph, first list each step or event in the correct order. When you write your paragraph, use sequence words and phrases to help the reader follow the order.

First, Initially, To begin with ➜ These sequence words and phrases are used to indicate the beginning of a process.

Second, Third, Then, Next, After, After that ➜ These sequence words and phrases show the following steps.

While, At the same time, During ➜ These sequence words and phrases show actions or steps that happen at the same time.

Finally, Last, Eventually ➜ These sequence words are used to indicate the final step.

Note: *When, As soon as,* and *Once* describe an event that happens just before another event.

First, *the water evaporates and turns into vapor that rises into the air.*
After that, *the water vapor turns back into a liquid.*

Once *the snowflakes become too heavy, they start to fall from the clouds.*
As soon as *the land surface temperature rises, the snow on the ground begins to melt.*

A process paragraph should be more than a list of steps. It is also important to include details that help the reader understand the steps or events.

D The sentences below describe the stages of a wildfire. Read the sentences and underline the sequence words or phrases. Then number the sentences (1–5) to put the stages in the correct order.

_____ Next, as the flames get bigger and spread farther, the fire reaches its hottest stage. At this point, the fire is fully developed.

_____ First, an ember[1] lands close to a fuel source, such as dry grass or leaves. As the ember reacts with oxygen, it increases in heat and strength.

_____ Finally, the fire is reduced to embers and ash. It often takes weeks to fully extinguish all the embers from a large fire.

_____ The combination of heat, oxygen, and fuel increases the likelihood of the fire growing to the second stage. This is when the fire begins to spread to the surrounding areas.

_____ Once all the fuel has been consumed, the fire begins to die out. However, any introduction of new fuel sources or an increase in oxygen can cause the fire to flare up again.

[1]An **ember** is a small piece of burning coal or wood.

E Now write the sentences from exercise D in the correct order to form a paragraph. Replace the underlined sequence words or phrases with others from the Writing Skill box.

When a wildfire starts, it goes through several different stages of growth. _____

_____

_____

_____

_____

_____

_____

_____

_____

_____

_____

_____

_____

WRITING TASK

GOAL You are going to write a paragraph on the following topic:

Explain a natural process that you know well. Choose one of the following or use your own idea:

- a volcanic eruption
- photosynthesis
- an earthquake
- a hurricane

TAKING NOTES **A** List a few natural or biological processes that you are familiar with. Do some research and take notes if necessary. Then try explaining the processes to a partner.

_____

_____

PLANNING **B** Follow these steps to plan your process paragraph.

Step 1 Choose a topic from your notes above and write it down in the outline below.

Step 2 List up to eight steps or events for your process in order in the outline. Don't worry about grammar or spelling. Don't write complete sentences.

Step 3 Write a topic sentence that introduces your process.

Step 4 Now write any details that will help the reader to better understand your steps or events.

OUTLINE

Topic: _____

Topic Sentence: _____

_____

Steps or Events	Details
1. _____	_____
2. _____	_____
3. _____	_____
4. _____	_____
5. _____	_____
6. _____	_____
7. _____	_____
8. _____	_____

FIRST DRAFT **C** Use the information in your outline to write a first draft of your paragraph.

REVISING PRACTICE

The drafts below are similar to the one you are going to write, but they are on a different topic:

Explain how a caterpillar turns into a monarch butterfly.

What did the writer do in Draft 2 to improve the paragraph? Match the changes (a–d) to the highlighted parts. Some can be used more than once.

a. added a detail to a step
b. added a sequence word or phrase
c. corrected a verb form
d. added a concluding sentence

Draft 1

The monarch butterfly has a life cycle that is different from that of most other insects. First, a monarch butterfly lay its eggs on a milkweed plant. After about four days, the eggs hatch into baby caterpillars. The caterpillars eat the milkweed in order to grow. When they are fully grown, they start the pupa stage. Each caterpillar attaches itself to a stem or a leaf and hangs upside down. It forms a chrysalis—a protective shell—around its body. Once it is in this chrysalis, its body begins to change. This transformation is called a metamorphosis. An adult butterfly flies out of the chrysalis and looks for a mate.

Draft 2

The monarch butterfly has a life cycle that is different from that of most other insects. First, a monarch butterfly lays its eggs on a milkweed plant. ☐
After about four days, the eggs hatch into baby caterpillars. As soon as they ☐
are born, the caterpillars eat the milkweed in order to grow. When they are fully grown, they start the pupa stage. Each caterpillar attaches itself to a stem or a leaf and hangs upside down. It forms a chrysalis—a protective shell—around its body. Once it is in this chrysalis, its body begins to change. It grows wings, legs, and other butterfly parts. This transformation is called a ☐
metamorphosis. After the metamorphosis, an adult butterfly flies out of the ☐
chrysalis and looks for a mate. This starts the cycle all over again. ☐

▲ **A monarch butterfly emerges from its chrysalis.**

D **Now use the questions below to revise your paragraph.**

REVISED DRAFT

☐ Does the topic sentence introduce the main idea?
☐ Are the steps in the correct order?
☐ Are there sequence words and phrases to show order?
☐ Are there detail sentences for some of the steps?
☐ Is there a concluding sentence?

FINAL DRAFT **E** Follow these steps to write a final draft.

1. Check your revised draft for mistakes with simple present verb forms.

2. Now use the checklist on page 79 to write a final draft. Make any other necessary changes.

UNIT REVIEW

Answer the following questions.

1. Which of the natural events in this unit would you like to know more about? Why?

_____

_____

2. What are three examples of sequence words or phrases that show order in a list of steps?

_____

_____

3. Do you remember the meanings of these words? Check (✓) the ones you know. Look back at the unit and review the ones you don't know.

Reading 1:

☐ climate   ☐ coast   ☐ collide

☐ condition   ☐ data AWL   ☐ extend

☐ occur AWL   ☐ on record   ☐ strike

☐ violent

Reading 2:

☐ appropriate AWL   ☐ block   ☐ frequent

☐ fuel   ☐ on purpose   ☐ particularly

☐ significant AWL   ☐ threaten

INVENTIVE SOLUTIONS 4

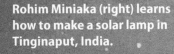

**Rohim Miniaka (right) learns
how to make a solar lamp in
Tinginaput, India.**

THINK AND DISCUSS

1 Do you know of any famous inventors? What
did they invent?
2 What inventions do you use every day?

A Look at the information on these pages and answer the questions.

  1. Do you agree with the list of the most important inventions? Can you think of other inventions to add?

  2. Of these top 10 inventions, how many were developed within the last 200 years? Why do you think this is?

B Match the words in blue to their definitions.

_____ (n) a plan or drawing that shows the look and function of something

_____ (adj) being effective without wasting time or energy

_____ (n) the tools, machines, and other items needed for a particular task

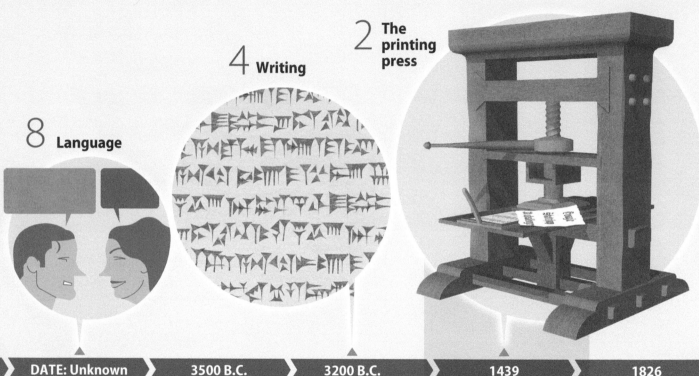

8 **Language**

4 **Writing**

2 **The printing press**

| DATE: Unknown | 3500 B.C. | 3200 B.C. | 1439 | 1826 |

3 **The wheel**

No one knows who invented the wheel, but historians believe that it first appeared in Mesopotamia around 3500 B.C. Today, wheels are used for transportation and in energy-generating **equipment**.

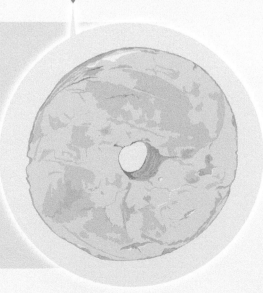

Johannes Gutenberg invented a new type of printing press in 1439. He based his **design** on existing technologies, but his invention had movable type. This made the printing process much faster. Soon, thousands of books were being printed on his presses throughout Europe, and later the world.

6 **The match**

WHAT'S THE WORLD'S GREATEST INVENTION?

The publishing company Raconteur asked over 400 people to name the world's most important inventions. Here are the top 10. Some inventions—like the car—make everyday life easier. Medical inventions—such as antibiotics— save lives. Others—like the smartphone— changed the way we communicate.

And the number one invention? According to survey results, the greatest invention of all time is the World Wide Web, followed by the printing press and the wheel.

5 **The motor car**

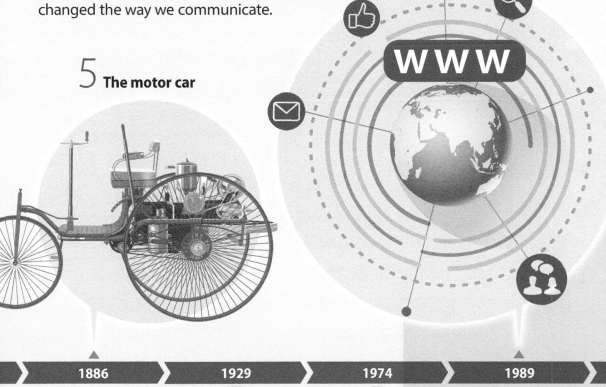

1 **The World Wide Web**

1886	1929	1974	1989	1992

In the 1980s, scientists at the European Organization for Nuclear Research (CERN) needed an **efficient** way to access each other's work. Tim Berners-Lee, a software engineer at CERN, created a system that made it easy to share information. In 1989, he had the idea of creating a similar system for the whole world. This became the World Wide Web—what most people today call "the Internet."

7 **Antibiotics**

9 **The personal computer**

10 **The smartphone**

Reading 1

PREPARING TO READ

BUILDING VOCABULARY

A The words in blue below are used in the reading passage on pages 63–64. Match the correct form of each word to its definition.

> **Electricity** has many uses—we cook with it, and heat and light our homes with it. It also **powers** our cell phones.
>
> Many people consider Thomas Edison—the inventor of the phonograph—to be one of the greatest **creative** thinkers of all time.
>
> Edison was partially deaf. He **struggled** to find a steady job before **eventually** becoming a famous inventor.
>
> Some inventions are very expensive, so not everyone can **afford** them.
>
> The French chemist Louis Pasteur is famous for his research on the causes and **prevention** of diseases.

1. _____ (v) to supply the energy needed for something to work

2. _____ (adv) in the end, especially after a lot of problems

3. _____ (n) a form of energy that can be used for heating and lighting

4. _____ (n) the act of making sure that something does not happen

5. _____ (v) to have enough money to pay for something

6. _____ (v) to try very hard to do something that is difficult

7. _____ (adj) able to invent things and have original ideas

USING VOCABULARY

B Discuss these questions with a partner.

1. Are you a **creative** person? Describe one way in which you are creative.
2. What are some sources of energy that can produce **electricity**?

BRAINSTORMING

C Make a list of things you use every day that require electricity. Share your ideas with a partner.

1. _____   3. _____   5. _____

2. _____   4. _____   6. _____

PREDICTING

D Skim the first paragraph of the reading passage on pages 63–64, and look at the pictures and captions. What do you think the reading passage is mainly about? Check your answer as you read.

a. energy shortages in Africa
b. a solution to an energy problem
c. how windmills generate electricity

THE POWER OF CREATIVITY

🎧 Track 5

A   William Kamkwamba lives in Malawi, Africa, where most people don't have access to **electricity** or running water.[1] They have to cook over open fires and collect water from wells or streams. Poverty is very high; only 2 percent of Malawians can **afford** electricity. In addition, most people have to grow their own food. Life is difficult there, and many people **struggle** to survive.

B   In 2001, when William was 14 years old, life in Malawi became even more difficult. There was a severe drought,[2] and most families—including William's—couldn't grow enough food. He explains, "Within five months all Malawians began to starve to death. My family ate one meal per day, at night."

C   Because of the drought, William's family couldn't afford to send him to school anymore. However, William wanted to continue his education, so he went to the library near his home one day. He found a science book there called *Using Energy*. It included instructions for building a windmill. Windmills can be very **efficient** sources of electricity, and they can bring water up from underground. William didn't know much English, and he wasn't able to understand most of the book, but it was full of pictures and diagrams.[3] Looking at the pictures, William thought he could build a windmill for his family.

[1]**Running water** is water that is brought into a building through pipes.
[2]A **drought** is a long period of time with no rain.
[3]**Diagrams** are drawings that show how something (e.g., a machine) works.

William Kamkwamba at a speaking event in 2013

William used old bicycle parts and other thrown-away items to build his windmill.

copper wire

tree branches

bicycle frame

tractor fan

Today, William's windmills are up to 12 meters tall.

D When William went home and started building his windmill, a lot of people in his village laughed at him, including his mother. They didn't think he could do it. However, William didn't let that stop him—he was confident. He saw the photo of the windmill in the book. That meant someone else was able to build it, so he knew he could build it, too. William was also creative. He didn't have the parts and equipment that he saw in the book's diagrams, and he couldn't buy them. So he looked for the parts that he needed in junkyards.[4]

E While building the windmill, William changed and improved his design little by little. At first, the windmill powered only one lightbulb. Then it powered four lights. Eventually, there was enough electricity for four lights and a radio. No one laughed at William after that, and people in his village started to come to his house to get power for their cell phones. Later, William built a second windmill. This one brought water up from underground. After that, he began to teach other people how to build windmills. He also continued to build more of them himself, including one at a primary school.

F Because of his success with the windmills, William was able to go back to school. He also helped to develop a malaria[5] prevention program and clean water services in his community. He wrote a book about his life called *The Boy Who Harnessed the Wind: Creating Currents of Electricity and Hope*. In addition, he uses his website to educate people and to give them hope. His main message is this: "To the Africans, and the poor who are struggling with your dreams ..., trust yourself and believe. Whatever happens, don't give up."

[4]A **junkyard** is a place where old machines are thrown away.
[5]**Malaria** is a disease spread by mosquitoes.

UNDERSTANDING THE READING

A Choose the best alternative title for the reading passage.

a. Windmills—Africa's Hope for the Future
b. Advice from a Young Inventor
c. The Boy Who Brought Electricity—and Hope

B Answer the questions below using information from the reading passage.

1. Why did life become very difficult for William's family in 2001?

_____

2. What did people in William's village think of his idea at first?

_____

3. How did William's first windmill help people in his village?

_____

> **CRITICAL THINKING** To **analyze problems and solutions** in a passage, ask yourself: Does the writer provide enough information to show why the problem is real? Is it clear how the solution matches the problem? If not, what solution(s) would you propose?

C Complete the chart below. Fill in the missing problems and solutions.

Problems				
William couldn't afford to go to school.	He couldn't read the book about windmills because he didn't know much English.		The village needed more water.	Other people wanted to build windmills but didn't know how.
↓	↓	↓	↓	↓

Solutions				
		William went to a junkyard.		

D Choose one of the problems mentioned in exercise C. In what other way(s) could William have dealt with it? Discuss with a partner.

DEVELOPING READING SKILLS

READING SKILL Identifying Details

Details tell more about the main idea. They explain, develop, and illustrate the author's main idea by giving reasons and examples. To help locate the details of a paragraph, first identify the main idea. Then turn the main idea statement into a question by using words like *who*, *what*, *when*, *where*, *why*, or *how*.

Look at the paragraph below from the reading passage. What does each colored sentence do?

When William went home and started building his windmill, a lot of people in his village laughed at him, including his mother. They didn't think he could do it. However, William didn't let that stop him—he was confident. He saw the photo of the windmill in the book. That meant someone else was able to build it, so he knew he could build it, too. William was also creative. He didn't have the parts and equipment that he saw in the book's diagrams, and he couldn't buy them. So he looked for the parts that he needed in junkyards.

The main idea of the paragraph is that William was confident and creative in building his windmill. The **red** sentences **give reasons** *why* William was confident. The **blue** sentences **give examples** of *how* William was creative.

IDENTIFYING THE MAIN IDEA AND DETAILS

A Read the information about seat belts. Then write the main idea of the paragraph and three details.

Many inventions change lives, but Nils Bohlin's invention has probably helped to save more than a million lives so far. Bohlin invented a new type of seat belt that is in most cars made today. Before Bohlin's invention, seat belts were buckled across the stomach. The buckles often caused injuries during high-speed accidents. Bohlin's seat belt holds the upper and lower body safely in place with one strap across the chest and one across the hips, with a buckle at the side.

Main Idea: _____

_____

Detail 1: _____

Detail 2: _____

Detail 3: _____

IDENTIFYING DETAILS

B Look back at the reading passage on pages 63–64. Find and underline three details. Then share your answers with a partner.

Video

Workers install solar electric panels on a roof in Camarillo, California.

SOLAR SOLUTIONS

BEFORE VIEWING

A What are some reasons for using solar power? Discuss your ideas with a partner.

PREDICTING

B Read the information about solar panels. Then answer the questions.

LEARNING ABOUT THE TOPIC

The energy from the sun's light is enough to fulfill all the world's power needs many times over. There are different ways to use this solar energy. The simplest method is to use solar hot water panels—these can be just boxes of hot water pipes covered with a glass sheet, usually placed on roofs. These turn the sun's visible light into infrared radiation. This heats water in copper pipes that can be used, for example, in a bathroom or kitchen. Solar electric panels, on the other hand, turn sunlight directly into electricity. These panels are made of special materials—such as silicon (made from sand), glass, and metal—that are expensive.

1. What is one advantage of solar power mentioned in the paragraph?

   _____

2. What two types of solar technology are mentioned? Which type do you think is more practical for use in developing countries and why?

   _____

   _____

C Below are some quotes from the video. Match the correct form of each **bold** word or phrase to its definition.

> "The garbage piled everywhere is considered valuable because it's often recycled and reused. Cairo has been **going green** long before it became fashionable."
>
> "The solar heaters allow urban **dwellers** access to a plentiful supply of hot water …, and they **cut down on** potential energy costs."
>
> "Once they accept that, solar is a **no-brainer** here. It's an easy thing to do."

1. _____ (v) to reduce or decrease

2. _____ (v) to live in an environmentally responsible way

3. _____ (n) something that is easy or obvious

4. _____ (n) a person who lives in a specific place

WHILE VIEWING

A ▶ Watch the video. Check (✓) the goals of Thomas Taha Culhane's project.

☐ 1. to bring affordable hot water to residents of Cairo
☐ 2. to show Egyptians how they can save water
☐ 3. to increase awareness about the importance of recycling

B ▶ Watch the video again and answer the questions below.

1. What are Culhane's solar-powered water heaters made from?

_____

2. Why is Cairo well-suited to Culhane's project?

_____

3. What is one problem with using solar panels in Cairo? What is a simple solution to this problem?

_____

AFTER VIEWING

A Discuss these questions with a partner.

1. Would solar-powered water heaters work well in your country? Why or why not?

2. What does the narrator say at the end of the video? Complete the sentence:

   "One man's _____ is another man's _____."

   What do you think this saying means?

B List two things William Kamkwamba's windmills and Thomas Taha Culhane's water heaters have in common.

_____

_____

Reading 2

PREPARING TO READ

A The words in blue below are used in the reading passage on pages 70–71. Read their definitions and then complete each sentence with the correct form of the word.

> A **container** is an object for holding or carrying something.
>
> An **innovation** is a new method, idea, or product.
>
> To **identify** means to be able to name someone or something.
>
> When you **store** something, you keep it for future use.
>
> A **device** is a piece of equipment made or adapted for a particular purpose.
>
> A **benefit** is a good or helpful result or effect.
>
> If something is **valuable**, it is of great use.
>
> To **indicate** means to point out or show something.

1. Research _____ that the global demand for energy is expected to triple by 2050.

2. One _____ of solar power is that it is renewable.

3. There have already been several technological _____ this century, such as the electric car and the tablet computer.

4. The wheel is one of the most _____ inventions of all time. Without it, we would probably have to walk or ride animals to travel long distances.

5. Before refrigerators were invented, people could not easily _____ fresh meat.

6. Blood tests and X-rays can help doctors _____ diseases.

7. Scientists can study the day-to-day movements of an animal by using a tracking _____.

8. Bottles are useful _____ for water and other liquids.

B Discuss these questions with a partner.

1. What are some recent **innovations** in healthcare?

2. Are there any new **devices** that you really want to get? If so, which ones?

C Skim the first paragraph of the reading passage on pages 70–71, and look at the photos and subheads. How might each item be useful? Discuss your ideas with a partner. Then check your ideas as you read the passage.

BIG IDEAS, LITTLE PACKAGES

A Can simple ideas change the world? They just might, one new idea at a time. Creative designers and scientists are working to invent products for communities in developing countries. Some of their innovations might solve even the biggest problems, such as improving access to healthcare and clean water.

INFANT WARMER

B Around 19 million low-birthweight babies are born every year in developing countries. These babies weigh less than 5.5 pounds (2.5 kilograms) when they're born. Low-birthweight babies often have difficulty staying warm because they don't have enough fat on their bodies. Many get too cold and die.

C To solve this problem, American entrepreneur Jane Chen and a team of people invented the Embrace infant warmer. It looks like a small sleeping bag and is specially designed to help keep babies warm. It's filled with wax that easily heats up to 37 degrees Celsius—the normal body temperature.[1] Another benefit of the Embrace infant warmer is that it can work without electricity. It's an easy-to-use, low-cost solution. To date, this simple invention has helped save more than 200,000 babies in Africa, Asia, and Latin America.

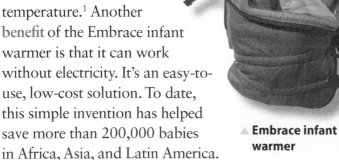

▲ **Embrace infant warmer**

[1] Your **body temperature** is how hot or cold your body is.

WATER CONTAINER

D Clean drinking water is one of the world's most valuable resources. Without it, people get sick and die. But getting clean water can be difficult for many people in developing countries. In poor areas, people often have to walk several miles to get clean water for cooking, cleaning, and drinking. They usually have to carry heavy containers of water on their heads. Most of them make several trips each day to collect water. This is difficult work, especially for women and children.

The Q Drum originated in response to the needs of rural people in South Africa.

HEALTH DETECTOR

F In many developing countries, doctors work with no electricity or clean water. They have to send medical tests to labs[2] and wait weeks for results. Patients may die while waiting to receive treatment. But a little piece of paper developed by Saudi Arabian scientist Hayat Sindi could change that.

G Sindi's device is only the size of a postage stamp, but it can help identify health problems. It contains tiny holes that are filled with chemicals. When a person places a single drop of blood on the paper, the chemicals react to the blood and cause the paper to change color. This indicates whether or not the person has an illness. Doctors can then take action immediately, saving time and lives. Since the health detector is made of paper, it's very light and easy to carry. Health workers can easily bring it with them to perform tests in patients' homes. Best of all, this can be done at a very low cost. No electricity, water, or special equipment is needed to use the device. Sindi explains, "It's a tool that allows even the poorest people in the most medically challenged places to get the tests they need."

[2]**Labs** are laboratories—places where scientific research is done.

E A South African engineer, Piet Hendrikse, came up with a solution to the problem of carrying water: the Q Drum. The Q Drum stores 13 gallons (about 50 liters) of water in a rolling container. Made of strong plastic material, it can roll over any kind of ground, no matter how rough. Anyone—even young children—can easily pull the drum with an attached rope. With this innovation, people in developing countries can carry more clean water per journey with less effort.

Hayat Sindi presents her invention at a 2009 conference.

UNDERSTANDING THE READING

UNDERSTANDING
MAIN IDEAS

A Choose the main purpose of each invention from the pairs of solution statements (a or b).

	Problem	Solution
Embrace Infant Warmer	Underweight babies have difficulty staying warm.	a. regulates body temperature of underweight babies b. measures body temperature and indicates when babies are cold
Q Drum	Many people in developing countries don't have easy access to clean water.	a. cleans water and makes it safe for cooking and drinking b. makes it easier for people to transport water
Health Detector	Doctors in remote areas don't have the equipment to process lab results.	a. helps doctors identify diseases quickly and accurately b. tells doctors what the best treatment is for a disease

IDENTIFYING
DETAILS

B Find details in the reading passage to answer each question below.

1. At what weight are babies considered low birthweight?

   _____

2. In developing countries, what is the traditional way of carrying water?

   _____

3. What is Hayat Sindi's health detector made of? What benefit does this have?

   _____

4. List two things the infant warmer, Q Drum, and health detector have in common.

   _____

CRITICAL THINKING:
EVALUATING

C If you gave an award for Best Invention, which of the four listed below would you choose? Consider:

How many people will it help? How much does it cost? Is it easy to make? Are there other inventions that fulfill the same need?

Check (✓) your winning invention. Note your reasons and share your decision with a partner.

☐ Solar-powered water heater   ☐ Q Drum water container

☐ Embrace infant warmer   ☐ Health detector

Reason(s): _____

_____

_____

UNIT REVIEW

Answer the following questions.

1. Which invention in this unit would you like to know more about? Why?

   _____

   _____

2. What details from the readings do you remember? Why?

   _____

   _____

3. Do you remember the meanings of these words? Check (✓) the ones you know. Look back at the unit and review the ones you don't know.

Reading 1:

☐ afford	☐ creative AWL	☐ design AWL
☐ efficient	☐ electricity	☐ equipment AWL
☐ eventually AWL	☐ power	☐ prevention
☐ struggle		

Reading 2:

☐ benefit AWL	☐ container	☐ device AWL
☐ identify AWL	☐ indicate AWL	☐ innovation AWL
☐ store	☐ valuable	

VOCABULARY EXTENSION   UNIT 1

WORD FORMS Changing Nouns and Adjectives into Verbs

The suffix -ize means "cause to become." Add -ize to some nouns and adjectives to make them into verbs. For nouns and adjectives ending in -y, drop the -y and add -ize.

ADJECTIVE	VERB
visual	visualize
NOUN	**VERB**
memory	memorize

A Complete each sentence using the verb form of a word from the box below.

> hospital   memory   modern   social   summary

1. I have a history test tomorrow. I need to _____ a lot of dates and names of places.

2. The community center is a good place for people to _____ with their neighbors.

3. The business will lose money if it doesn't _____ and adopt new technology.

4. A good reading comprehension strategy is to _____ the article in your own words.

5. A doctor may quickly _____ a patient if that patient needs immediate medical care.

WORD PARTNERS Expressions with *state*

Below are definitions for common expressions with the word *state*.

state of affairs: a situation or set of circumstances

state of emergency: a severe situation in which the government has increased powers to deal with a problem

state of repair: the physical condition of something (e.g., a building)

state of shock: the condition of being very upset because of something unexpected

state-of-the-art: the best available or the newest

B Complete the information using the expressions from the box above.

According to a recent report, the average age of a typical American public school building is 44 years. Some of these schools are in a bad [1]_____—broken roofs, doors, and windows. Other schools have poor lighting and heating systems. This [2]_____ can lead to poor student performance.

Many people are in a [3]_____ over the poor condition of American public schools. The cost of improving these schools is estimated to be about $145 billion. Unfortunately, many school districts already face funding shortfalls. Some authorities have declared a [4]_____ in their school districts. More investment is needed to turn these public schools into modern, [5]_____ centers of learning.

VOCABULARY EXTENSION   UNIT 3

The prefix *ex-* can mean "from" or "out of." For example, *extend* means "to stretch out from one place to another."

A   Complete each sentence using the correct form of a word from the box below.

> exit   explain   explore   export   extend

1. After the airplane landed, the passengers _____ the plane through the front door.

2. The Amazon River _____ from the mountains of Peru to the coast of Brazil.

3. Many cavers have _____ the Krubera Cave—the world's deepest cave—in Georgia.

4. Scientists cannot fully _____ why some storms form into massive hurricanes and other storms don't.

5. Japan manufactures a large number of cars. In 2016, it _____ over $90 billion worth of cars to other countries around the world.

WORD FORMS   Changing Adjectives into Adverbs

Many adverbs are formed by adding *-ly* to the end of adjectives. For adjectives ending in *-le*, replace the final *-e* with *-y*. For adjectives ending in *-y*, remove the final *-y* and add *-ily*.

ADJECTIVE	ADVERB
frequent	*frequently*
appropriate	*appropriately*
possible	*possibly*
easy	*easily*

B   Circle the correct adjective or adverb in each sentence to complete the paragraph.

A [1]**particular / particularly** bad winter storm hit Argentina in July 2007. Snow fell in Buenos Aires for the first time in 89 years—an [2]**extreme / extremely** rare event. In [3]**remote / remotely** areas of the country, over 60 cm of snow fell. Temperatures were also [4]**significant / significantly** below normal. In the province of Rio Negro, temperatures dropped to –22 degrees Celsius. The storm left at least 46 people [5]**dead / deadly** in Argentina.

VOCABULARY EXTENSION UNIT 4

Below are definitions for common collocations with the word *power*.

full power: the maximum amount of power that something can produce

solar power: electricity produced using energy from the sun

power failure: a loss of the electric power to a particular area

power line: a cable that carries electricity into a building

power plant: a building or group of buildings where electricity is produced

A Match the sentence parts in the columns to complete each sentence.

_____ 1. Some countries are building large nuclear   a. full power.

_____ 2. The storm brought down trees that cut several   b. solar power.

_____ 3. It takes a few minutes for the machine to reach   c. power plants.

_____ 4. The lights aren't working—there must be a   d. power failure.

_____ 5. A popular form of renewable energy is   e. power lines.

Some adjectives end with the suffix *-able* or *-ible*, which means "able to." Adjectives formed from nouns and verbs often end in *-able* (e.g., *comfort—comfortable*). If the noun or verb ends in *-e*, drop the *-e* and add *-able* (e.g., *advise—advisable*).

Other adjectives not formed from nouns and verbs usually end in *-ible* (e.g., *incredible*).

B Circle the correct form of the word to complete each sentence.

1. Advances in technology have made many low-cost innovations **possable / possible**.

2. A patent—the exclusive legal right to make or sell an invention for a limited period of time—can be a very **valueable / valuable** business asset.

3. Most mobile apps are **compatable / compatible** with different smartphone models.

4. The baby-warmer invention is an **affordable / affordible** solution for developing countries.

5. Space travel became technologically **feasable / feasible** in the twentieth century.

GRAMMAR REFERENCE

UNIT 1
Language for Writing: Using *By* + Gerund

Spelling Rules for Forming Gerunds

When forming gerunds, follow these rules for adding *-ing* to verbs:

1. Most verbs: Add *-ing*:

   sleep → sleeping   think → thinking   remember → remembering

2. Verbs that end with a consonant followed by *-e*: Drop the *-e* and add *-ing*:

   memorize → memorizing   store → storing   use → using

   By using *effective marketing techniques, companies can attract more customers.*

3. One-syllable verbs ending with a consonant + vowel + consonant: Double the final consonant and add *-ing*:

   get → getting   stop → stopping   put → putting

   (Exceptions: verbs that end in *-w*, *-x*, or *-y*; for example, say → saying)

   You can get into college **by getting** *good grades.*

4. Two-syllable verbs ending with a consonant + vowel + consonant, where the second syllable is stressed: Double the final consonant and add *-ing*:

   admit → admitting   begin → beginning   prefer → preferring

Language for Writing: Review of the Simple Past Tense

Affirmative and Negative Statements with *Be*

Affirmative Statements			Negative Statements		
Subject	*Was/Were*		Subject	*Was/Were Not*	
I He She It	**was**	happy. busy. a doctor. a student. online. at home.	I He She It	**was not wasn't**	happy. busy. a doctor. a student. online. at home.
You We They	**were**		You We They	**were not weren't**	

Affirmative and Negative Statements: Other Verbs

Affirmative Statements		Negative Statements		
Subject	Verb (Past Form)	Subject	*Did Not*	Verb (Base Form)
I You We They He She It	**started** a project. **walked** home. **studied**. **went** to school.	I You We They He She It	**did not didn't**	**start** a project. **walk** home. **study**. **go** to school.

Past Forms of Commonly Used Irregular Verbs

become—became begin—began bring—brought build—built buy—bought choose—chose do—did eat—ate	fall—fell find—found get—got give—gave have—had hear—heard know—knew make—made	read—read say—said see—saw speak—spoke take—took tell—told think—thought write—wrote

EDITING CHECKLIST

Use the checklist to find errors in your writing task for each unit.

	WRITING TASK	
	1	2
1. Is the first word of every sentence capitalized?		
2. Does every sentence end with the correct punctuation?		
3. Do your subjects and verbs agree?		
4. Are commas used in the right places?		
5. Do all possessive nouns have an apostrophe?		
6. Are all proper nouns capitalized?		
7. Is the spelling of places, people, and other proper nouns correct?		
8. Did you check for frequently confused words?		

Brief Writer's Handbook

Understanding the Writing Process: The Seven Steps

The Assignment

Imagine that you have been given the following assignment: *Write a definition paragraph about an everyday item.*

What should you do first? What should you do second, third, and so on? There are many ways to write, but most good writers follow certain general steps in the writing process.

Look at this list of steps. Which ones do you usually do? Which ones have you never done?

STEP 1: Choose a topic.

STEP 2: Brainstorm.

STEP 3: Outline.

STEP 4: Write the first draft.

STEP 5: Get feedback from a peer.

STEP 6: Revise the first draft.

STEP 7: Proofread the final draft.

Now you will see how one student went through all the steps to do the assignment. First, read the final paragraph that Susan gave her teacher. Read the teacher's comments as well.

Example Paragraph 1

Gumbo

The dictionary definition of *gumbo* does not make gumbo sound as delicious as it really is. The dictionary defines gumbo as a "thick soup made in south Louisiana." However, anyone who has tasted this delicious dish knows that this definition is too bland to describe gumbo. It is true that gumbo is a thick soup, but it is much more than that. Gumbo, one of the most popular of all Cajun dishes, is made with different kinds of seafood or meat mixed with vegetables, such as green peppers and onions. For example, seafood gumbo contains shrimp and crab. Other kinds of gumbo include chicken, sausage, or turkey. Regardless of the ingredients in gumbo, this regional delicacy is very delicious.

Teacher comments:

100/A⁺   Excellent paragraph!

I enjoyed reading about gumbo. Your paragraph is very well written. All the sentences relate to one single topic. I really like the fact that you used so many connectors—however, such as.

Now look at the steps that Susan went through to compose the paragraph that you just read.

Steps in the Writing Process
Step 1: Choose a Topic
Susan chose gumbo as her topic. This is what she wrote about her choice.

○   When I first saw the assignment, I did not know what to write about. I did not think I was going to be able to find a good topic.
    First, I tried to think of something that I could define. It could not be something that was really simple like television or a car. Everyone already knows what they are. I thought that I should choose something that most people might not know.
    I tried to think of general areas like sports, machines, and inventions. However, I chose food as my general area. Everyone likes food.

○   Then I had to find one kind of food that not everyone knows. For me, that was not too difficult. My family is from Louisiana, and the food in Louisiana is special. It is not the usual food that most Americans eat. One of the dishes we eat a lot in Louisiana is gumbo, which is a kind of thick soup. I thought gumbo would be a good topic for a definition paragraph because not many people know it, and it is sort of easy for me to write a definition for this food.
    Another reason that gumbo is a good choice for a definition paragraph is that I know a lot about this kind of food. I know how to make it, I know what the ingredients are, and I know what it tastes like. It is much easier to write about something that I know than about something that I do not know about.

○   After I was sure that gumbo was going to be my topic, I went on to the next step, which is brainstorming.

**Susan's notes about
choosing her topic**

Step 2: Brainstorm

The next step for Susan was to brainstorm ideas about her topic.

In this step, you write down every idea that pops into your head about your topic. Some of these ideas will be good, and some will be bad—write them all down. The main purpose of brainstorming is to write down as many ideas as you can think of. If one idea looks especially good, you might circle that idea or put a check mark next to it. If you write down an idea and you know right away that you are not going to use it, you can cross it out.

Look at Susan's brainstorming diagram on the topic of gumbo.

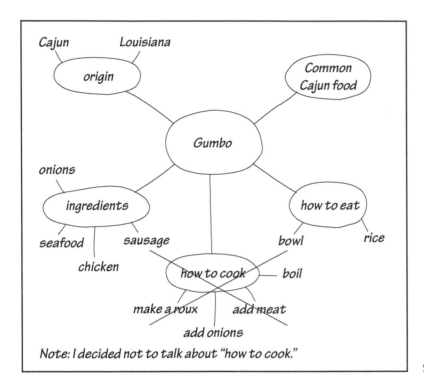

Susan's brainstorming diagram

Step 3: Outline

At this point, some writers want to start writing, but that is not the best plan. After you brainstorm your ideas, the next step is to make an outline. An outline helps you organize how you will present your information. It helps you see which areas of the paragraph are strong and which are weak.

After brainstorming, Susan studied her list of ideas. She then made a simple outline of what her paragraph might look like. Some writers prepare very detailed outlines, but many writers just make a list of the main points and some of the details for each main point.

Read the outline that Susan wrote.

What is gumbo?
1. A simple definition of gumbo.
2. A longer definition of gumbo.
3. A list of the different ingredients of gumbo.
   A. seafood or meat
   B. with vegetables (onions)
   C. seafood gumbo
4. How gumbo is served.

Susan's outline

As you can see, this outline is very basic. There are also some problems. For example, Susan repeats some items in different parts of the outline. In addition, she does not have a concluding sentence. These errors will probably be corrected at the first draft step, the peer editing step, or the final draft step.

Step 4: Write the First Draft

Next, Susan wrote a first draft. In this step, you use the information from your outline and from your brainstorming session to write a first draft. This first draft may contain many errors, such as misspellings, incomplete ideas, and incorrect punctuation. At this point, do not worry about correcting the errors. The main goal is to put your ideas into sentences.

You may feel that you do not know what you think about the topic yet. In this case, it may be difficult for you to write, but it is important to start the process of writing. Sometimes writing helps you think, and as soon as you form a new thought, you can write it down.

Read Susan's first draft, including her notes to herself.

Introduction is weak ??? Use dictionary!

(Rough draft)
Susan Mims

Do you know what gumbo is. It's a seafood soup. However, gumbo is really more than a kind of soup, it's special. ???

○ *Gumbo is one of the most popular of all Cajun dish.* es

Combine { *It's made with various kind of seafood or meet. meat*
This is mixed with vegetables such as onions. green peppers

Combine { *Seafood Gumbo is made with shrimp and crab.*
Also chicken, sausage, and turkey, etc. Regardless ok ???
of what is in Gumbo, it's usually served in bowl over the rice. a
— *Is this correct? Ask teacher!*

○

Susan's first draft

What do you notice about this first draft? Here are a few things that a good writer should pay attention to:

- First of all, remember that this paper is not the final draft. Even native speakers who are good writers usually write more than one draft. You will have a chance to revise the paper and make it better.

- Look at the circles, question marks, and writing in the margin. These are notes that Susan made to herself about what to change, add, or reconsider.

- Remember that the paper will go through the peer-editing process later. Another reader will help you make your meaning clear and will look for errors.

In addition to the language errors that writers often make in the first draft, the handwriting is usually not neat. Sometimes it is so messy that only the writer can read it!

Step 5: Get Feedback from a Peer

Peer editing a draft is a critical step toward the final goal of excellent writing. Sometimes it is difficult for writers to see the weaknesses in their own writing, so receiving advice from another writer can be very helpful.

Ask a colleague, friend, or classmate to read your writing and to offer suggestions about how to improve it. Some people do not like criticism, but constructive criticism is always helpful for writers. Remember that even professional writers have editors, so do not be embarrassed to receive help.

Susan exchanged papers with another student, Jim, in her class. On the next page is the peer editing sheet that Jim completed about Susan's paragraph. Read the questions and answers.

Peer Editing Sheet

Writer: _Susan_   Date: _2-14_

Peer Editor: _Jim_

1. What is the general topic of the paper? _gumbo_

2. What is the writer's purpose? (in 15 words or less)

   to define gumbo

3. Is the paragraph indented? ☑ yes   ❏ no

4. How many sentences are there? _6_

5. Is the first word of every sentence capitalized? ☑ yes   ❏ no
   If you answered *no,* circle the problem(s) on the paper.

6. Does every sentence end with correct punctuation? ❏ yes   ☑ no
   If you answered *no,* circle the problem(s) on the paper.

7. Are there any other capitalization or punctuation errors? ☑ yes   ❏ no
   If you answered *yes,* circle the problem(s) on the paper.

8. Write the topic sentence here.

   You have two sentences: Do you know what gumbo is. It is a seafood soup.

9. Do you think the topic sentence is good for this paragraph? Comments?

   No, you need one sentence that introduces your topic and purpose better.

10. Does the paragraph talk about just one topic? ☑ yes   ❏ no

    If you answered *no,* what is the extra topic? _____

    In what sentence is this extra topic introduced? _____

11. Does every sentence have a verb? ☐ yes ☑ no

If you answered *no*, circle the error(s) on the paper.

12. Write any mistakes that you found. Add appropriate corrections.

Error 1: _it's-don't use contractions in formal writing_

Correction: _it is_

Error 2: _etc.-don't use this_

Correction: _You should list all the kinds._

Error 3: _____

Correction: _____

13. Did you have any trouble understanding this paragraph? ☐ yes ☑ no

If you answered *yes*, tell where and/or why.

_____

14. What questions do you have about the content? What other information should be in this paragraph?

How do you make gumbo? Is it easy to cook? Why do you think people started making gumbo?

15. What is your opinion of the writing of this paragraph?

It is good, but the concluding sentence gives new information. It does not conclude! Also,

do not repeat the word "gumbo" so much. Do not use "is" so much! Use other verbs.

16. What is your opinion of the content of this paragraph?

I like the topic. I think I ate gumbo at a restaurant once.

Step 6: Revise the First Draft

In this step, you will see how Susan used the suggestions and information to revise her paragraph. This step consists of three parts:

1. React to the comments on the peer editing sheet.

2. Reread the paragraph and make changes.

3. Rewrite the paragraph one more time.

Here is what Susan wrote about the changes she decided to make.

> I read my paragraph again several times. Each time I read it, I found things that I wanted to change in some way. Sometimes I corrected an obvious error. Other times I added words to make my writing clear to the reader. Based on Jim's suggestion, I used "this delicious dish" and other expressions instead of repeating "gumbo" so many times.
>
> I used some of Jim's suggestions, but I did not use all of them. I thought that some of his questions were interesting, but the answers were not really part of the purpose of this paragraph, which was to define gumbo.
>
> I was happy that the peer editor was able to understand all my ideas fully. To me, this means that my writing is good enough.

Susan's notes about changes she decided to make

Step 7: Proofread the Final Draft

Most of the hard work should be over by now. In this step, the writer pretends to be a brand-new reader who has never seen the paper before. The writer reads the paper to see if the sentences and ideas flow smoothly.

Read Susan's final paper again on page 80. Notice any changes in vocabulary, grammar, spelling, or punctuation that she made at this stage.

Of course, the very last step is to turn the paper in to your teacher and hope that you get a good grade!

Editing Your Writing

While you must be comfortable writing quickly, you also need to be comfortable with improving your work. Writing an assignment is never a one-step process. For even the most gifted writers, it is often a multiple-step process. When you were completing your assignments in this book, you probably made some changes to your work to make it better. However, you may not have fixed all of the errors. The paper that you turned in to your teacher is called a **first draft,** which is sometimes referred to as a **rough draft.**

A first draft can almost always be improved. One way to improve your writing is to ask a classmate, friend, or teacher to read it and make suggestions. Your reader may discover that one of your paragraphs is missing a topic sentence, that you have made grammar mistakes, or that your essay needs different vocabulary choices. You may not always like or agree with the comments from a reader, but being open to changes will make you a better writer.

This section will help you become more familiar with how to identify and correct errors in your writing.

Step 1

Below is a student's first draft for a timed writing. The writing prompt for this assignment, was "Many schools now offer classes online. Which do you prefer and why?" As you read the first draft, look for areas that need improvement and write your comments. For example, does every sentence have a subject and a verb? Does the writer always use the correct verb tense and punctuation? Does the paragraph have a topic sentence with controlling ideas? Is the vocabulary suitable for the intended audience? What do you think of the content?

The Online Courses

Online courses are very popular at my university. I prefered traditional face-to-face classes. At my university, students have a choice between courses that are taught online in a virtual classroom and the regular kind of classroom. I know that many students prefer online classes, but I cannot adjust to that style of educate. For me, is important to have a professor who explains the material to everyone "live" and then answer any questions that we have. Sometimes students might think they understand the material until the professor questions, and then we realize that we did not understand everything. At that moment, the professor then offers other explanation to help bridge the gap. I do not see this kind of spontaneous learning and teaching can take place online. I have never taken an online course until now. Some of my friends like online courses because they can take the class at his own convenience instead of have to assist class at a set time. However, these supposed conveniences are not outweigh the educational advantages that traditional face-to-face classes offer.

Step 2

Read the teacher comments on the first draft of "The Online Courses." Are these the same things that you noticed?

Your title is OK. Any other ideas?

The Online Courses

Combine first two sentences.

Online courses are very popular at my university. I prefered traditional face-to-face

classes. At my university, students have a choice between courses that are taught online in a virtual

Give more details about CLASS3ROOM. Describe it.

classroom and the regular kind of classroom. I know that many students prefer online classes,

WORD FORM SUBJ?

but I cannot adjust to that style of educate. For me, is important to have a professor who explains

the material to everyone "live" and then answer any questions that we have. Sometimes students

POSES A QUESTION

might think they understand the material until the professor questions, and then we realize that

we did not understand everything. At that moment, the professor then offers other explanation

Which gap???   HOW?

to help bridge the gap. I do not see this kind of spontaneous learning and teaching can take place

Purpose of this sentence? Connected to the topic?

online. I have never taken an online course until now. Some of my friends like online courses

because they can take the class at his own convenience instead of have to assist class at a set

Add more reasons here!

time. ∧ However, these supposed conveniences are not outweigh the educational advantages that

traditional face-to-face classes offer.

You have some very good ideas in this paragraph. Your topic sentence and concluding sentence are good. Your title is OK, but can you spice it up? It's rather plain right now. Check to make sure that all of your sentences are relevant. Also, I've circled several grammar errors. You need to change these. I also recommend adding some info in a few places. All in all, it's a good paragraph. I understand why you don't like online courses. The more specific reasons you can provide, the better you can convince your readers.

Step 3

Now read the writer's second draft of the paragraph. How is it the same as the first draft? How is it different? Did the writer fix all the sentence mistakes?

Online Courses

Online courses are very popular at my university but I prefer traditional face-to-face classes. At my university students have a choice between courses that are taught online in a virtual classroom and the regular kind of classroom with a room, a professor, and students in chairs. I know that many students prefer online classes, but I cannot adjust to that style of education. For me, it is important to have a professor who explains the material to everyone "live" and then answers any questions that we might have. Sometimes students might think they understand the material until the professor poses a question, and then we realize that we did not understand everything. At that moment, the professor then offers another explanation to help bridge the gap between our knowledge and the truth. I do not see how this kind of spontaneous leaerning and teaching can take place online. Some of my friends like online courses because they can take the class at their own convenience instead of having to attend class at a set time. They also like to save transportation money and time. However, these supposed conveniences do not outweigh the many educational advantages that traditional face-to-face classes offer.

Read the following paragraph. Circle the capitalization errors and make corrections above the errors.

Example Paragraph 2

A visit to Cuba

according to an article in last week's issue of *time*, the prime minister of canada will visit cuba soon in order to establish better economic ties between the two countries. because the united states does not have a history of good relations with cuba, canada's recent decision may result in problems between washington and ottawa. In an interview, the canadian prime minister indicated that his country was ready to reestablish some sort of cooperation with cuba and that canada would do so as quickly as possible. there is no doubt that this new development will be discussed at the opening session of congress next tuesday.

ACTIVITY 5

Read the following paragraph. Circle the capitalization errors and make corrections above the errors.

Example Paragraph 3

crossing the atlantic from atlanta

it used to be difficult to travel directly from atlanta to europe, but this is certainly not the case nowadays. union airways offers several daily flights to london. jetwings express offers flights every day to frankfurt and twice a week to berlin. other european air carriers that offer direct flights from atlanta to europe are valuair and luxliner. However, the airline with the largest number of direct flights to any european city is not a european airline. smead airlines, which is a new and rising airline in the united states, offers 17 flights a day to 12 european cities, including paris, london, frankfurt, zurich, rome, and athens.

Read the following paragraph. Circle the capitalization errors and make corrections above the errors.

my beginnings in foreign languages

      I have always loved foreign languages. When I was in tenth grade, I took my first foreign language class. It was french I. My teacher was named mrs. montluzin. She was a wonderful teacher who inspired me to develop my interest in foreign languages. Before I finished high school, I took a second year of french and one year of spanish. I wish my high school had offered latin or greek, but the small size of the school body prevented this. Over the years since I graduated from high school, I have lived and worked abroad. I studied arabic when I lived in saudi arabia, japanese in japan, and malay in malaysia. Two years ago, I took a german class in the united states. Because of recent travels to uzbekistan and kyrgyzstan, which are two republics from the former soviet union, I have a strong desire to study russian. I hope that my love of learning foreign languages will continue.

Punctuation Activities
End Punctuation

      The three most common punctuation marks found at the end of English sentences are the **period**, the **question mark**, and the **exclamation point**. It is important to know how to use all three of them correctly. Of these three, however, the period is by far the most commonly used punctuation mark.

1. **period** (.) A period is used at the end of a declarative sentence.

    This sentence is a declarative sentence.

    This sentence is not a question.

    All three of these sentences end with a period.

2. **question mark** (?) A question mark is used at the end of a question.

    Is this idea difficult?

    Is it hard to remember the name of this mark?

    How many questions are in this group?

3. **exclamation point** (!) An exclamation point is used at the end of an exclamation. It is less common than the other two marks.

> I cannot believe you think this topic is difficult!

> This is the best writing book in the world!

> Now I understand all of these examples!

ACTIVITY 1

Add the correct end punctuation.

1. Congratulations

2. Do most people think that the governor was unaware of the theft

3. Do not open your test booklet until you are told to do so

4. Will the president attend the meeting

5. Jason put the dishes in the dishwasher and then watched TV

ACTIVITY 2

Look at an article in any English newspaper or magazine. Circle every end punctuation mark. Then answer these questions.

1. How many final periods are there? _____ (or _____ %)

2. How many final question marks are there? _____ (or _____ %)

3. How many final exclamation points are there? _____ (or _____ %)

4. What is the total number of sentences? _____

Use this last number to calculate the percentages for each of the categories. Does the period occur most often?

Commas

The comma has several different functions in English. Here are some of the most common ones.

1. A comma separates a list of three or more things. There should be a comma between the items in a list.

> He speaks French and English. (No comma is needed because there are only two items.)

> She speaks French, English, and Chinese.

2. A comma separates two sentences when there is a combining word (coordinating conjunction) such as *and, but, or, so, for, nor,* and *yet.* The easy way to remember these conjunctions is *FANBOYS (for, and, nor, but, or, yet, so).*

> Six people took the course, but only five of them passed the test.

> Sammy bought the cake, and Paul paid for the ice cream.

> Students can register for classes in person, or they may submit their applications by mail.

3. A comma is used to separate an introductory word or phrase from the rest of the sentence.

> In conclusion, doctors are advising people to take more vitamins.

> First, you will need a pencil.

> Because of the heavy rains, many of the roads were flooded.

> Finally, add the nuts to the batter.

4. A comma is used to separate an appositive from the rest of the sentence. An appositive is a word or group of words that renames a noun before it. An appositive provides additional information about the noun.

subject (noun)   appositive   verb

Washington, the first president of the United States, was a clever military leader.

In this sentence, the phrase *the first president of the United States* is an appositive. This phrase renames or explains the noun *Washington*.

5. A comma is sometimes used with adjective clauses. An adjective clause usually begins with a relative pronoun *(who, that, which, whom, whose, whoever,* or *whomever)*. We use a comma when the information in the clause is unnecessary or extra. (This is also called a nonrestrictive clause.)

The book <u>that is on the teacher's desk</u> is the main book for this class.

(Here, when you say "the book," the reader does not know which book you are talking about, so the information in the adjective clause is necessary. In this case, do not set off the adjective clause with a comma.)

The History of Korea, <u>which is on the teacher's desk,</u> is the main book for this class.

(The name of the book is given, so the information in the adjective clause is not necessary to help the reader identify the book. In this case, you must use commas to show that the information in the adjective clause is extra, or nonrestrictive.)

ACTIVITY 3

Add commas as needed in these sentences. Some sentences may be correct, and others may need more than one comma.

1. For the past fifteen years Mary Parker has been both the director and producer of all the plays at this theater.

2. Despite all the problems we had on our vacation we managed to have a good time.

3. I believe the best countries to visit in Africa are Senegal Tunisia and Ghana.

4. She believes the best countries to visit in Africa are Senegal and Tunisia.

5. The third step in this process is to grate the carrots and the potatoes.

6. Third grate the carrots and the potatoes.

7. Blue green and red are strong colors. For this reason they are not appropriate for a living room wall.

8. Without anyone to teach foreign language classes next year the school will be unable to offer French Spanish or German.

9. The NEQ 7000 the very latest computer from Electron Technologies is not selling very well.

10. Because of injuries neither Carl nor Jamil two of the best players on the football team will be able to play in tomorrow's game.

11. The job interview is for a position at Mills Trust Company which is the largest company in this area.

12. The job interview is for a position at a large company that has more than 1,000 employees in this area.

13. Kevin's birthday is January 18 which is the same day that Laura and Greg have their birthdays.

14. Martina Navratilova whom most tennis fans refer to only as Martina dominated women's tennis for years.

15. My brother who lives in San Salvador has two children. (I have several brothers.)

16. My brother who lives in San Salvador has two children. (I have only one brother.)

17. This flight is leaving for La Paz which is the first of three stops that the plane will make.

18. No one knows the name of the person who will take over the committee in January so there have been many rumors about this.

19. Greenfield Central Bank the most recent bank to open a branch here in our area has tried to establish a branch here for years.

20. On the right side of the living room an antique radio sits on top of a glass table that also has a flowerpot a photo of a baby and a magazine.

Apostrophes

Apostrophes have two basic uses in English. They indicate either a contraction or possession.

Contractions: Use an apostrophe in a contraction in place of the letter or letters that have been deleted.

> He's (he is *or* he has), they're (they are), I've (I have), we'd (we would *or* we had)

Possession: Use an apostrophe to indicate possession. Add an apostrophe and the letter *s* after the word. If a plural word already ends in *s*, then just add an apostrophe.

> Gandhi's role in the history of India
> Yesterday's paper
> the boy's books (One boy has some books.)
> the boys' books (Several boys have one or more books.)

ACTIVITY 4

Correct the apostrophe errors in these sentences.

1. I am going to Victors birthday party on Saturday.

2. My three cousins house is right next to Mr. Wilsons house.

3. Hardly anyone remembers Stalins drastic actions in the early part of the last century.

4. It goes without saying that wed be better off without so much poverty in this world.

5. The reasons that were given for the childrens bad behavior were unbelievable.

Quotation Marks

Below are three of the most common uses for quotation marks.

1. To mark the exact words that were spoken by someone:

    The king said, "I refuse to give up my throne." (The period is inside the quotation marks.)*

    "None of the solutions is correct," said the professor. (The comma is inside the quotation marks.)*

    The king said that he refuses to give up his throne. (No quotation marks are needed because the sentence does not include the king's exact words. This style is called indirect speech.)

    * Note that the comma separates the verb that tells the form of communications (*said, announced, wrote*) and the quotation.

2. To mark language that a writer has borrowed from another source:

    The dictionary defines gossip as an "informal conversation, often about other people's private affairs," but I would add that it is usually malicious.

    This research concludes that there was "no real reason to expect this computer software program to produce good results with high school students."

    According to an article in *The San Jose Times,* about half of the money was stolen. (No quotes are necessary here because it is a summary of information rather than exact words from the article.)

3. To indicate when a word or phrase is being used in a special way:

    The king believed himself to be the leader of a democracy, so he allowed the prisoner to choose his method of dying. According to the king, allowing this kind of "democracy" showed that he was indeed a good ruler.

ACTIVITY 5

Add quotation marks where necessary. Remember the rules for placing commas, periods, and question marks inside or outside the quotation marks.

1. As I was leaving the room, I heard the teacher say, Be sure to study Chapter 7.

2. It is impossible to say that using dictionaries is useless. However, according to research published in the latest issue of the *General Language Journal,* dictionary use is down. I found the article's statement that 18.3 percent of students do not own a dictionary and 37.2 percent never use their dictionary (p. 75) to be rather shocking.

    Source: Wendt, John "Dictionary Use by Language Students," *General Language Journal* 3 (2007): 72-101.

3. My fiancée says that if I buy her a huge diamond ring, this would be a sign that I love her. I would like to know if there is a less expensive sign that would be a sure sign of my love for her.

4. When my English friend speaks of a heat wave just because the temperature reaches over 80°, I have to laugh because I come from Thailand, where we have sunshine most of the year. The days when we have to dress warmly are certainly few, and some people wear shorts outside almost every month of the year.

5. The directions on the package read, Open carefully. Add contents to one glass of warm water. Drink just before bedtime.

Semicolons

The semicolon is used most often to combine two related sentences. Once you get used to using the semicolon, you will find that it is a very easy and useful punctuation tool to vary the sentences in your writing.

- Use a semicolon when you want to connect two simple sentences.

- The function of a semicolon is similar to that of a period. However, in order to use a semicolon, there must be a relationship between the sentences.

> Joey loves to play tennis. He has been playing since he was ten years old.

> Joey loves to play tennis; he has been playing since he was ten years old.

Both sentence pairs are correct. The main difference is that the semicolon in the second example signals the relationship between the ideas in the two sentences. Notice also that *he* is not capitalized in the second example.

ACTIVITY 6

The following sentences use periods for separation. Rewrite the sentences. Replace the periods with semicolons and make any other necessary changes.

1. Gretchen and Bob have been friends since elementary school. They are also next-door neighbors.

   _____

2. The test was complicated. No one passed it.

   _____

3. Tomatoes are necessary for a garden salad. Peas are not.

   _____

4. Mexico lies to the south of the United States. Canada lies to the north.

   _____

Look at a copy of an English newspaper or magazine. Circle all the semicolons on a page. The number should be relatively small.

NOTE: If the topic of the article is technical or complex, there is a greater chance of finding semicolons. Semicolons are not usually used in informal or friendly writing. Thus, you might see a semicolon in an article about heart surgery or educational research, but not in an ad for a household product or an e-mail or text message to a friend.

Editing for Errors

ACTIVITY 8

Find the 14 punctuation errors in this paragraph and make corrections above the errors.

Example Paragraph 5

An Unexpected Storm

Severe weather is a constant possibility all over the globe; but we never really expect our own area to be affected However last night was different At about ten o'clock a tornado hit Lucedale This violent weather destroyed nine homes near the downtown area In addition to these nine houses that were completely destroyed many others in the area had heavy damage Amazingly no one was injured in last nights terrible storm Because of the rapid reaction of state and local weather watchers most of the areas residents saw the warnings that were broadcast on television

ACTIVITY 9

Find the 15 punctuation errors in this paragraph and make corrections above the errors.

Example Paragraph 6

Deserts

Deserts are some of the most interesting places on earth A desert is not just a dry area it is an area that receives less than ten inches of rainfall a year About one-fifth of the earth is composed of deserts Although many people believe that deserts are nothing but hills of sand this is not true In reality deserts have large rocks mountains canyons and even lakes For instance only about ten percent of the Sahara Desert the largest desert on the earth is sand

ACTIVITY 10

Find the 15 punctuation errors in this paragraph and make corrections above the errors.

Example Paragraph 7

A Review

I Wish I Could Have Seen His Face Marilyn Kings latest novel is perhaps her greatest triumph In this book King tells the story of the Lamberts a poor family that struggles to survive despite numerous hardships. The Lambert family consists of five strong personalities. Michael Lambert has trouble keeping a job and Naomi earns very little as a maid at a hotel The three children range in age from nine to sixteen. Dan Melinda and Zeke are still in school This well-written novel allows us to step into the conflict that each of the children has to deal with. Only a writer as talented as King could develop five independent characters in such an outstanding manner The plot has many unexpected turns and the outcome of this story will not disappoint readers While King has written several novels that won international praise *I Wish I Could Have Seen His Face* is in many ways better than any of her previous works.

Additional Grammar Activities
Verb Tense

ACTIVITY 1

Fill in the blanks with the verb that best completes the sentence. Be sure to use the correct form of the verb. Use the following verbs: *like, cut, break, stir,* and *spread.*

Example Paragraph 8

A Simple Sandwich

Making a tuna salad sandwich is not difficult. Put two cans of flaked tuna in a medium-sized bowl. With a fork, _____ the fish apart. _____ up a large white onion or two small yellow onions. _____ in one-third cup of mayonnaise. Then add salt and pepper to taste. Some people _____ to mix

pieces of boiled eggs into their salad. Once you finish making the salad,

_____ it between two slices of bread. Now you are ready to

eat your easy-to-make treat.

ACTIVITY 2

Fill in the blanks with the correct form of any appropriate verb.

Example Paragraph 9

Who Killed Kennedy?

One of the most infamous moments in U.S. history _____

in 1963. In that year, President John F. Kennedy _____

assassinated in Dallas, Texas. Since this event, there _____

many theories about what _____ on that fateful day.

According to the official U.S. government report, only one man

_____ the bullets that _____ President

Kennedy. However, even today many people _____ that

there _____ several assassins.

ACTIVITY 3

Fill in the blanks with the correct form of any appropriate verb.

Example Paragraph 10

A Routine Routine

I have one of the most boring daily routines of anyone I

_____ . Every morning, I _____ at 7:15.1

_____ a shower and _____ dressed.

After that, I _____ breakfast and _____

to the office. I _____ from 8:30 to 4:30. Then I

_____ home. This _____ five days a week

without fail. Just for once, I wish something different would happen!

Fill in the blanks with the correct form of the verbs in parentheses.

Example Paragraph 11

The Shortest Term in the White House

William Henry Harrison (be) _____ the ninth
president of the United States. His presidency was extremely brief.
In fact, Harrison (be) _____ president for only one
month. He (take) _____ office on March 4,1841.
Unfortunately he (catch) _____ a cold that (become)
_____ pneumonia. On April 4, Harrison (die)
_____ . He (become) _____ the first
American president to die while in office. Before becoming president,
Harrison (study) _____ to become a doctor and later
(serve) _____ in the army.

ACTIVITY 5

Fill in the blanks with the correct form of the verbs in parentheses.

Example Paragraph 12

The History of Brownsville

Brownsville, Texas, is a city with an interesting history. Brownsville
(be) _____ originally a fort during the Mexican-
American War. During that war, American and Mexican soldiers (fight)
_____ several battles in the area around the city. As a
matter of fact, the city (get) _____ its name from Major
Jacob Brown, an American soldier who was killed in a battle near the
old fort. However, Brownsville's history (be) _____
not only connected to war. After the war, the city was best known for
farming. The area's rich soil (help) _____ it become
a thriving agriculture center. Over time, the agricultural industry
(grow) _____ , and today Brownsville farmers (be)
_____ well-known for growing cotton and citrus. In sum,
both the Mexican-American War and farming have played important
historical roles in making Brownsville such an interesting city.

Articles

Fill in the blanks with the correct article. If no article is required, write an X in the blank.

Example Paragraph 13

_____ Simple Math Problem

There is _____ interesting mathematics brainteaser that always amazes _____ people when they first hear it. First, pick _____ number from _____ 1 to _____ 9. Subtract _____ 5. (You may have a negative number.) Multiply this answer by _____ 3. Now square _____ number. Then add _____ digits of _____ number. For _____ example, if your number is 81, add 8 and 1 to get an answer of _____ 9. If _____ number is less than _____ 5, add _____ 5. If _____ number is not less than _____ 5, subtract _____ 4. Now multiply this number by _____ 2. Finally, subtract _____ 6. If you have followed _____ steps correctly, _____ your answer is _____ 4.

Fill in the blanks with the correct article. If no article is required, write an X in the blank.

Example Paragraph 14

_____ Geography Problems among _____ American Students

Are _____ American high school students _____ less educated in _____ geography than high school students in _____ other countries? According to _____ recent survey of _____ high school students all over _____ globe, _____ U.S. students do not know very much about _____ geography. For _____

example, _____ surprisingly large number did not know

_____ capital of _____ state in which

they live. Many could not find _____ Mexico on a map

even though Mexico is one of _____ two countries

that share _____ border with _____

United States. Some _____ educators blame this lack of

_____ geographical knowledge on the move away from

memorization of material that has taken _____ place

in _____ recent years in American schools. Regardless

of _____ cause, the unfortunate fact appears to be that

American _____ high school students are not learning

enough about this subject area.

ACTIVITY 8

Fill in the blanks with the correct article. If no article is required, write an X in the blank.

Example Paragraph 15

_____ Homeowners Saving _____ Money with a New Free Service

People who are concerned that their monthly electricity

bill is too high can now take _____ advantage of

_____ special free service offered by the local electricity

company. _____ company will do _____

home energy audit on any house to find out if _____

house is wasting _____ valuable energy. Homeowners

can call _____ power company to schedule _____

convenient time for _____ energy analyst to visit

their home. The audit takes only about _____ hour.

_____ analyst will inspect _____

home and identify potential energy-saving _____

improvements. For _____ example, he or she will

check _____ thermostat, the air-conditioning, and

_____ seals around doors and windows. The major

energy-use _____ problems will be identified, and

_____ analyst will recommend _____

ways to use _____ energy more efficiently.

ACTIVITY 9

Fill in the blanks with the correct article. If no article is required, write an X in the blank.

_____ Great Teacher

To this day, I am completely convinced that _____ main reason that I did so well in my French class in _____ high school was the incredible teacher that I had, _____ Mrs. Montluzin. I had not studied _____ foreign language before I started _____ Mrs. Montluzin's French class. _____ idea of being able to communicate in a foreign language, especially _____ French, intrigued me, but _____ idea also scared me. _____ French seemed so difficult at first. We had so much _____ vocabulary to memorize, and we had to do _____ exercises to improve our grammar. While it is true that there was _____ great deal of work to do, _____ Mrs. Montluzin always tried her best to make French class very interesting. She also gave us _____ suggestions for learning _____ French, and these helped me a lot. Since this French class, I have studied a few other languages, and my interest in _____ foreign languages today is due to _____ success I had in French class with _____ Mrs. Montluzin.

ACTIVITY 10

Fill in the blanks with the correct article. If no article is required, write an X in the blank.

_____ Surprising Statistics on _____ Higher Education in _____ United States

Although _____ United States is a leader in many areas, it is surprising that _____ number of Americans with _____ college degree is not as high as it is in some _____ other countries. Only about 22 percent of

_____ Americans have attended college for four or more

years. To _____ most people, this rather low ratio of one

in five is shocking. Slightly more than _____ 60 percent

of _____ Americans between _____

ages of 25 and 40 have taken some _____ college classes.

Though these numbers are far from what _____ many

people would expect in _____ United States, these

statistics are _____ huge improvement over figures

at _____ turn of _____ last century.

In _____ 1900, only about _____ 8

percent of all Americans even entered _____ college. At

_____ present time, there are about 21 million students

attending _____ college.

Editing for Errors

ACTIVITY 11

This paragraph contains eight errors. They are in word choice (one), article (one), modal* (one), verb tense (one), subject-verb agreement (three), and word order (one). Mark these errors and write the corrections above the errors.

Example Paragraph 18

A Dangerous Driving Problem

Imagine that you are driving your car home from mall or the library. You come to a bend in the road. You decide that you need to slow down a little, so you tap the brake pedal. Much to your surprise, the car does not begin to slow down. You push the brake pedal all the way down to the floor, but still anything happens. There are a few things you can do when your brakes does not work. One was to pump the brakes. If also this fails, you should to try the emergency brake. If this also fail, you should try to shift the car into a lower gear and rub the tires against the curb until the car come to a stop.

*Modals are *can, should, will, must, may,* and *might.* Modals appear before verbs. We do not use *to* between modals and verbs. (*Incorrect:* I should to go with him. *Correct:* I should go with him.) Modals do not have forms that take *-s, -ing,* or *-ed.*

This paragraph contains ten errors. They are in prepositions (three), word order (one), articles (two), and verb tense (four). Mark these errors and write the corrections above the errors.

The Start of My Love of Aquariums

My love of aquariums began a long time ago. Although I got my first fish when I am just seven years old, I can still remember the store, the fish, and salesclerk who waited on me that day. Because I made good grades on my report card, my uncle has rewarded me with a dollar. A few days later, I was finally able to go to the local dime store for spend my money. It was 1965, and dollar could buy a lot. I looked a lot of different things, but I finally chose to buy a fish. We had an old fishbowl at home, so it seems logical with me to get a fish. I must have spent 15 minutes pacing back and forth in front of all the aquariums before I finally choose my fish. It was a green swordtail, or rather, she was a green swordtail. A few weeks later, she gave birth to 20 or 30 baby swordtails. Years later, I can still remember the fish beautiful that got me so interested in aquariums.

This paragraph contains eight errors. They are in prepositions (one), articles (three), word forms (two), verb tense (one), and subject-verb agreement (one). Mark these errors and write the corrections above the errors.

An Effect of Cellphones on Drivers

Cellular phones, can be threat to safety. A recent study for Donald Redelmeier and Robert Tibshirani of the University of Toronto showed that cellular phones pose a risk to drivers. In fact, people who talk on the phone while driving are four time more likely to have an automobile accident than those who do not use the phone while drive. The Toronto researchers studied 699 drivers who had been in an automobile accident while they were using their cellular phones. The researchers concluded that the main reason for the accidents is not that people used one hand for the telephone and only one for driving. Rather, cause of the accidents was usually that the drivers became distracted, angry, or upset by the phone call. The drivers then lost concentration and was more prone to a car accident.

This paragraph contains seven errors. They are in verb tense (one), articles (two), word forms (three), and subject-verb agreement (one). Mark these errors and write the corrections.

Example Paragraph 21

Problems with American Coins

Many foreigners who come to the United States have very hard time getting used to America coins. The denominations of the coins are one, five, ten, 25, and 50 cents, and one dollar. However, people used only the first four regularly. The smallest coin in value is the penny, but it is not the smallest coin in size. The quarter is one-fourth the value of a dollar, but it is not one-fourth as big as a dollar. There is a dollar coin, but no one ever use it. In fact, perhaps the only place to find one is at a bank. All of the coins are silver-colored except for one, the penny. Finally, because value of each coin is not clearly written on the coin as it is in many country, foreigners often experience problems with monetarily transactions.

ACTIVITY 15

This paragraph contains seven errors. They are in word order (one), articles (two), preposition (one), subject-verb agreement (one), and verb tense (two). Mark these errors and write the corrections.

Example Paragraph 22

An Oasis of Silence

Life on this campus can be extremely hectic, so when I want the solitude, I go usually to the fourth floor of the library. The fourth floor has nothing but shelves and shelves of rare books and obscure periodicals. Because there are only a few small tables with some rather uncomfortable wooden chairs and no copy machines in this floor, few people are staying here very long. Students search for a book or periodical, found it, and then take it to a more sociable floor to photocopy the pages or simply browse through the articles. One of my best friends have told me that he does not like this floor that is so special to me. For him, it is a lonely place. For me, however, it is oasis of silence in a land of turmoil, a place where I can read, think, and write in peace.

Useful Vocabulary for Better Writing

These useful words and phrases can help you write better sentences and paragraphs. They can make your writing sound more academic, natural, and fluent.

Giving and Adding Examples

Words and Phrases	Examples
For example, S + V / For instance, S + V	Our reading teacher assigns a lot of homework. *For example*, last night we had to read ten pages and write an essay.
The first reason + VERB	The article we read in class gave three reasons that our planet is in trouble. *The first reason* is about the increasing population.

Concluding Sentences

Words and Phrases	Examples
In conclusion, S + V	*In conclusion*, I believe everyone should vote in every election.
By doing all of these things, S + V	*By doing all of these things*, we can improve education in our country.
Because of this, S + V	*Because of this*, many people will have better health care.
As a result, S + V	*As a result*, I chose to go to college in France instead of my country.
For these reasons, S + V	*For these reasons*, I prefer to eat at home instead of a restaurant.
In sum, S + V / In summary, S + V / To summarize , S + V	*In sum*, World War II was a very complicated war with many countries fighting for very different reasons, but in many ways, it was a continuation of World War I.
In other words, S + V	*In other words*, the judge made an incorrect decision.
From the information given, we can conclude that S + V	*From the information given, we can conclude that* Mark Johnson is certainly the best soccer player in this decade.
It is clear that S + V	*It is clear that* exercising every day improved your health.

Comparing

Words and Phrases	Examples
NOUN *is* COMPARATIVE ADJECTIVE *than* NOUN	New York *is larger than* Rhode Island.
S + V + COMPARATIVE ADVERB *than* Y.	The cats ran *faster than* the dogs.
S + V. In comparison, S + V.	Canada has provinces. *In comparison*, Brazil has states.
Although NOUN *and* NOUN *are similar in* NOUN, S + V	*Although* France *and* Spain *are similar in* size, they are different in many ways.
NOUN *and* NOUN *are similar.*	Brazil *and* the United States *are* surprisingly *similar.*
NOUN *is the same*	Our house *is the same* size as your house.
…as ADJECTIVE *as…*	Our house is *as big as* your house.
Like NOUN, NOUN *also*	*Like* Brazil, Mexico *also* has states.
both NOUN *and* NOUN…	*In both* German *and* Japanese, the verb appears at the end of a sentence.

Likewise, S + V / Also, S + V	The blooms on the red roses last longer than most other flowers. *Likewise*, the blooms for the pink rose are long-lasting.
Similarly, S + V …/ Similar to NOUN	Economists believe India has a bright future. *Similarly*, Brazil's future is on a very positive track.

Contrasting

Words and Phrases	Examples
S + V. *In contrast,* S + V.	*Algeria* is a very large country. *In contrast,* the UAE is very small.
Contrasted with / In contrast to NOUN	*In contrast to* last year, our company has doubled its profits this year.
Although / Even though / Though S + V	*Although* Spain and France are similar in size, they are different in many other ways.
Unlike NOUN,	*Unlike* the pink roses, the red roses are very expensive.
However, S + V	Canada has provinces. *However,* Brazil has states.
On the one hand, S + V On the other hand, S + V	*On the one hand,* Maggie loved to travel. *On the other hand,* she hated to be away from her home.
The opposite S + V	Most of the small towns in my state are experiencing a boom in tourism. In my hometown, *the opposite* is true.
NOUN *and* NOUN *are different.*	My older brother *and* my younger brother *are very different.*

Telling a Story / Narrating

Words and Phrases	Examples
When I was X, I would VERB	*When I was* a child, *I would* go fishing every weekend.
I have never felt so ADJ in my life.	*I have never felt so* anxious *in my life.*
I will never forget NOUN	*I will never forget* the day I took my first international flight.
I can still remember NOUN / I will always remember NOUN	*I can still remember* the day I started my first job.
NOUN was the best / worst day of my life.	My wedding was *the best day of my life.*
Every time X happened, Y happened.	*Every time* I used that computer, I had a problem.
This was my first …	*This was my first* job after graduating from college.

Describing a Process

Words and Phrases	Examples
First (Second, Third, etc.), … Next,… After that,…Then,… Finally,…	*First,* I cut the apples into small pieces. *Next,* I added some mayonnaise. *After that,* I added some salt. *Finally,* I mixed everything together well.
The first thing you should do is VERB	*The first thing you should do is* turn on the computer.
VERB+-ing requires you to follow (number) of steps.	*Saving* a file on a computer *requires you to follow several simple steps.*
Before you VERB, you should VERB.	*Before you* write a paragraph, *you should* brainstorm for ideas.
After (When)…	*After* you brainstorm your ideas, you can select the best ones to write about in your essay.

After that, ...	After that, you can select the best ones to write about in your essay.
The last step is… / Finally, ...	Finally, you should cook all of the ingredients for an hour.
If you follow these important steps in VERB + -ing,…	If you follow these important steps in applying for a passport, you will have your new document in a very short time.

Defining

Words and Phrases	Examples
The NOUN, which is a/an NOUN + ADJECTIVE CLAUSE, MAIN VERB	An owl, which is a bird that has huge round eyes, is awake most of the night.
According to the dictionary…	According to The Collins Cobuild Dictionary of American English, gossip is "an informal conversation, often about people's private affairs."
The dictionary definition of NOUN	The dictionary definition of gumbo is not very good.
X released a report stating that S + V	The president's office released a report stating that the new law will require all adults between the ages of 18 and 30 to serve at least one year of active military duty.
In other words, S + V	In other words, we have to redo everything we have done so far.
,…which means…	The paper is due tomorrow, which means if you want to get a good grade, you need to finish it today.
NOUN means…	Gossip means talking or writing about other people's private affairs.

Showing Cause and Effect

Words and Phrases	Examples
Because of NOUN, S + V. Because S + V, S + V.	Because of the traffic problems, it is easy to see why the city is building a new tunnel.
NOUN can trigger NOUN. NOUN can cause NOUN.	An earthquake can trigger tidal waves and can cause massive destruction.
Due to NOUN, ...	Due to the snowstorm, all schools will be closed tomorrow.
As a result of NOUN…	As a result of his efforts, he got a better job.
Therefore,…/ As a result,…/ For this reason,…/ Consequently,…	It suddenly began to rain. Therefore, we all got wet.
NOUN will bring about ...	The use of the Internet will bring about a change in education.
NOUN has had a good / bad effect on…	Computer technology has had both positive and negative effects on society.
The correlation is clear / evident.	The correlation between junk food and obesity is clear.

Describing

Words and Phrases	Examples
Prepositions of location: *above, across, around, in the dark, near, under…*	The children raced their bikes *around* the school.
Descriptive adjectives: *wonderful, delightful, dangerous, informative, rusty…*	The *bent, rusty* bike squeaked when I rode it.
SUBJECT *is* ADJECTIVE.	This dictionary *is informative*.
X is the most ADJECTIVE + NOUN.	To me, Germany *is the most interesting* country in Europe.
X tastes / looks / smells / feels like NOUN.	My ID card *looks like* a credit card.
X is known / famous for its NOUN.	France *is known for* its cheese.

Stating an Opinion

Words and Phrases	Examples
Without a doubt, VERB *is* ADJECTIVE *idea / method / decision / way.*	*Without a doubt,* walking to work each day *is* an excellent *way* to lose weight.
Personally, I believe/think/feel/agree/ disagree/ suppose S + V.	*Personally, I believe that* smoking on a bus should not be allowed.
VERB+*-ing should not be allowed.*	Smoking in public *should not be allowed.*
In my opinion/ view/ experience, NOUN	*In my opinion,* smoking is rude.
For this reason, S + V. / *That is why I think…*	I do not have a car. *For this reason,* I do not care about rising gasoline prices.
There are many benefits / advantages to NOUN.	*There are many benefits* to swimming every day.
There are many drawbacks / disadvantages to NOUN.	*There are many drawbacks* to eating your meals at a restaurant.
I am convinced that S + V	*I am convinced that* education at a university should be free to all citizens.
NOUN *should be required / mandatory.*	College *should be required.*
I prefer NOUN *to* NOUN.	*I prefer* soccer to football.
To me, banning / prohibiting NOUN *makes (perfect) sense.*	*To me, banning* cell phones while driving *makes perfect sense.*
For all of these important reasons, I think / believe / feel (that) S + V	*For all of these important reasons, I think* smoking *should be* banned in public.
Based on X, I have come to the conclusion that S + V	*Based on* two books that I read recently, *I have come to the conclusion that* global warming is the most serious problem that my generation faces.

Arguing and Persuading

Words and Phrases	Examples
It is important to remember that S + V	*It is important to remember* that school uniforms would only be worn during school hours.
According to a recent survey, S + V	*According to a recent survey,* 85 percent of high school students felt they had too much homework.
Even more important, S + V	*Even more important,* statistics show the positive effects that school uniforms have on behavior.
Despite this, S + V	The report says this particular kind of airplane is dangerous. *Despite this,* the government has not banned this airplane.
SUBJECT *must / should / ought to* VERB	Researchers *must* stop unethical animal testing.
The reason for S + V	*The reason for* people's support of this plan is that it provides equal treatment for all citizens.
To emphasize, S + V	*To emphasize,* I support a lower age for voting but only for those who already have a high school diploma.
For these reasons, S + V	*For these reasons,* public schools should require uniforms.
Obviously, S + V	*Obviously,* there are many people who would disagree with what I have just said.
Without a doubt, S + V	*Without a doubt,* students ought to learn a foreign language.
I agree that S + V. *However* S + V	*I agree that* a college degree is important. *However,* getting a practical technical license can also be very useful.

Reacting/Responding

Words and Phrases	Examples
TITLE *by* AUTHOR *is a / an...*	*Harry Potter and the Goblet of Fire by* J.K. Rowling *is an* entertaining book to read.
My first reaction to the prompt / news / article was / is NOUN.	*My first reaction to the article was* fear.
When I read / look at / think about NOUN, *I was amazed / shocked / surprised ...*	*When I read* the article, *I was surprised* to learn of his athletic ability.

NOTES

NOTES

NOTES

NOTES

NOTES

NOTES

NOTES

NOTES

NOTES

NOTES